THE NEW RADICALISM
Anarchist or Marxist?

The

NEW RADICALISM:

Anarchist or Marxist?

by GIL GREEN

INTERNATIONAL PUBLISHERS
New York

322.42
G79ᵧ n

NOTE ON REFERENCES

References in the text are given in abbreviated form, either by author
or by title: if reference is made to more than one book by the same
author, the date of publication is given. The page numbers of the work
cited in the text refer to the book or anthology in which the work
appears. Full details of publication of the cited work are given in the
Bibliography at the end of the volume.

Library of Congress Catalog Card Number: 78-163220
ISBN (Cloth) 7178-0321-X; (paperback) 7178-0322-8
Printed in the United States of America

CONTENTS

CHAPTER I

YOUTH IN REVOLT

THE MASSIVE youth revolt that has been with us for more than a decade is one of the most remarkable phenomena of our time, without historic parallel. What seemed at first to be just a new youthful fad soon to go the way of all fads has turned out to be far more than a passing fancy.

It is the young radicals who deserve the main credit for having broken through the stifling, complacent and conformist mood of a decade ago. They have confronted the Establishment on a thousand different fronts, with a freshness, vigor, imagination and audacity beautiful to behold. They have shouted for all to hear that the king is naked and now more and more people see—and admit—that this is so.*

In a sense there has always been and will always be some form of youth revolt. No two generations are identical; each faces problems distinctly its own. Even old problems reappear wearing new garb.

Youth in the Fifties was known as the "Silent Generation." Yet it was by no means all silent, any more than was the generation of the Sixties all vocal, or that of the early Seventies all radical. Silence does not always imply consent. Sometimes it is a period of quiet incubation from which a new articulation emerges.

---

*"American young people are disillusioned these days. The kids do feel the lights have gone out in Camelot; the parade is over; the banners are furled." (U.S. Attorney, Thomas A. Foran, in his closing argument to the jury in the Chicago Conspiracy Trial, *New York Times*, February 14, 1970.)

"Behind all the questions of politics, ideologies and personalities . . . lies the larger issue of public confidence and trust in the institutions of the nation. . . . That trust does not exist now. The authority of the Government, of the church, of the university, and even of the family is under challenge all over the Republic, and men of all ages, stations and persuasions agree that this crisis of confidence is one of the most important and dangerous problems of the age." (James Reston, *New York Times*, April 8, 1970.)

7

In the Fifties too there were youth who were turned off by the society of their elders and who chose the beatnik pad, thereby becoming the unknowing forerunners of the later-day hippies. It was in the early Sixties that young activists began to make news again, rejecting the McCarthy era and its Cold War mentality, and fervently entering the struggles for civil rights and peace as the two great moral issues of the day.

But the present-day rebellion of so many young people is not just a repetition of the age-old generational problem. It has a scope, dimension and quality quite different from any revolt of the past. Today, everything is questioned and challenged; nothing is accepted at face value. The style of the rebellion is also different, with methods often bordering on the shockingly absurd and bizarre.

What explains the impassioned revolt of a large portion of the young generation and for so long a period of time?

In the Thirties this country also witnessed a convulsive youth upheaval. It was the period of the "unwanted generation," when young people could find no work in factory, field, office or profession. The youth upsurge was a direct outgrowth of the years of bitter class conflict. It was part, therefore, of a more universal people's insurgence and did not take on the same generational overtones as that of today. Young and old alike were responding to an economic breakdown which directly and intimately affected them both.

Conditions in the Sixties were quite different. On the surface, at least, and up to recently, the system seemed to be operating at its productive best—if by best is meant the avoidance of a massive economic breakdown such as that of the Thirties. But the new radicalism refuses to use this as the yardstick for judging the system, even if many of the older generation, still haunted by old memories, continue to do so.

A considerable proportion of youth is not impressed with the system's ability to produce. It is appalled at *how* this is being done, at the role of armaments, the military and war, and at the cost in human life and human values. Nor is it impressed by the mountains of junk and gadgetry produced. And it is incensed and aroused at the gross, irresponsible violation of the necessary mutual relationship between man and his natural environment.

The new radicals know that material well-being has improved for many. But this too leaves them cold. They are aware that poverty has increased side by side with affluence and that hunger is still the lot of all too many, particularly of Black, Brown, Red and Yellow peoples of this country and the world.

What shocks them most of all is the realization that the latest revolution in science and technology makes possible a society in which the essential needs of all can be met without excessive toil, drudgery, or long hours of labor. Yet they see technology not as a neutral friend but as a monstrous demonic foe, running completely amuck, turning man into a mere cog devoid of individuality, and threatening the very extinction of life on earth.

This is the first generation to reach the moon. It is also the first to be alarmingly aware that science can also be used to kill and to kill in a hundred different ways and on a scale never known before.

The youth consciousness produced by the upsurge of the Thirties was not counterposed to the growing class consciousness of the time, but tended to merge with it. Today's brand of youth consciousness is different. It tends to think of youth as a separate class, even an oppressed class, and if not a class, at least a caste. This is not as true of minority youth for whom the mainspring of rebellion is the racial oppression of their people. Yet to one degree or another the vast majority of youth today feel a special kinship with each other, flowing from dissatisfaction with the world as it is and with the ways of their parents.

It is as if the most intelligent and sensitive of white middle-class youth had looked into the mirror of their own family lives and recoiled in horror at what they saw. No, never! It would not happen to them! They would not succumb to the venality, hypocrisy, callousness and petty concern with trivia that so characterized the lives of their parents.

When men live and earn their living in the same way from generation to generation, the age gap is narrow; the new respects the old and accepts its more experienced, more mature judgment.

But when the world undergoes radical and rapid change for which there is no precedence; when the world no longer resembles the one described in school textbooks or discussed by parents, teachers or clergy; when man's relations to nature, society and his fellow men are being fundamentally altered, then the young generation no longer finds its guideposts in the past. It seeks to hew its own way forward, discarding all advice, the good along with the bad.

In this sense, Vice President Spiro Agnew is not entirely wrong when he blames TV and newspaper coverage—yes, the corporate controlled media—for stirring passions and rebellious moods. But to the degree he is right it is for the wrong reason. Try as the media do to edit and slant the news, they cannot completely block from youth's vision the existence of a barbaric, genocidal war in Indochina, the poverty and oppression of the ghetto, and the general corruption and decay of the society all around them.

It is especially among college youth that the modern mode of youth consciousness takes on its more extreme forms and its own life style. A number of developments account for this. First, the ongoing revolution in science and technology demands a young generation with much greater scientific, technical and professional skill. This has a tendency to contract the relative size of the industrial work force. Under conditions of relative prosperity this has resulted in larger numbers of working class sons and daughters going to college. Another factor swelling college enrollment has been the desire to escape the draft. Thus the number of college and university students has nearly tripled in the past two decades and multiplied nearly seven-fold since the Thirties.

Whole new communities, even small cities, have mushroomed around the universities. It is now commonplace for the large state colleges to have student enrollments of 25,000 to 45,000 in both graduate and undergraduate matriculating studies. The age band called "youth" has now been expanded to include graduate students well into the upper twenties and even thirties. With some 50 per cent of the nation's total population under 25 years of age, the youth category is indeed a sizeable chunk of the whole.

Students live crowded into their own communities, sharing

close, even intimate, living experiences with other young people, reinforcing their feeling of separation from productive life and the "outside world." Paul Goodman, in his book *Like A Conquered Province,* refers to "such collections of youth" as "a social phenomenon unique in history" (p. 32). Unique in history is also the fact that the young today are the first generation to grow up with knowledge of "the pill." This has brought on a revolution in sex mores and has given the young, particularly women, a sense of physical freedom never experienced before. In turn it has further widened the life-style gap between the generations.

The most knowledgeable and most sophisticated of the students also share a common revulsion to the meaningless and/or reactionary character of many of the studies required of them and the hypocritical notion that a college degree is a true measure of learning. Continued aid from parents, at the same time that there is frequent estrangement from them, creates its own kind of tension and even gets translated into a sensation of oppression. In time, the reality of this rarefied artificial existence creates its own false consciousness: it begins to think of itself as the real world and the real world as the anti-world. And from all this arises a life style meant to bolster this illusion and an elitist approach to ordinary people who must work if they are to eat.

They are accustomed to living in their own communities, often afraid to face up to the problems of the real world. These communities then become perpetuated in other forms, frequently as ghettoized extensions of the college community itself. A conscious attempt is made to link up and identify with another category of youth who also do not work, the unemployed ghetto youth. But there is a world of difference between being born in a ghetto or slum from which one cannot escape and just visiting there. Like the reformer who spends a night in the county jug for the sake of "experience," he can never experience what it is to be a lifer!

There is still one other important difference between the youth upsurge of the Thirties and that of today. The movement of the Thirties, like that of the Sixties, also had its origin in and was constantly replenished by mighty gushers of spontaneous protest.

But what distinguished it from today's movement is that those spontaneous outpourings were successfully channelled into the building of great popular mass organizations involving millions. In a sense this was inherent in the basically working-class character of the upheaval. Working people know from bitter experience that without disciplined organization they are helpless in any fight with the highly organized and centralized power of capital and its governmental machine. There was also then a more effective, better oragnized Left, determined to harness the elemental force of spontaneity for more permanent ends.

Today's movement is different. The wonderful outbursts of spontaneous protest with their many highly imaginative forms of struggle have not led to the formation of new, great popular organizations of the people. Leaders come and leaders go in endless procession. New organizations and ad hoc committees proliferate, but they are here today and gone tomorrow. Few of the new organizations have displayed great staying power and none are free of internal dissension and crisis.

The spontaneous movement, despite periods of lull and passivity, continues to spread to ever wider circles of people despite the fractured and split state of its organized sectors. And anyone who has had contact with the young still in high school knows that they are far more rebellious than anything yet seen.

The new radicalism has had no fixed ideology. It has been for the most part certainly Left, although amorphously so. This too has been somewhat inevitable. The elemental, massive character of the revolt, the completely new conditions that gave it birth, its separation in time and style from the radicalism of the Thirties, and its highly mixed class background in which middle-class influence predominates, greatly determined its ideological stance. Spontaneity could produce no more than it did—a hybrid type of eclectic thinking passed off by some as "no ideology" and by others as "new ideology."

Lack of consistent world outlook and perspective have become the movement's greatest weakness. Unless youth's seething restlessness finds expression in an ideology consistent with historic needs, its immense vitality and potentiality will become diffuse and dissipated.

Two distinct tendencies have characterized the new radicalism from the outset. These have existed side by side and have cross-fertilized each other. One tendency sought to build a solid, growing, serious movement for change. The other saw the movement in purely individualistic terms, as an outlet for personal frustrations and a place where individuals can do their thing—anything. The spokesmen for this latter trend see the movement as the stage and they the actors in a theater of the absurd. They are out to change society by "dropping out," by seeking to escape to their own rarefied, slum, utopian, psychedelic counter-communities. They are voluntary outcasts, the new breed of self-imposed untouchables, who by their clothes, appearance, language and total life style aim shockingly to demonstrate that society is not for them and they not for society.

Escape from society is no more possible than from gravity. Even men under conditions of spatial weightlessness must still depend upon links with earth for survival. When it comes to doing battle, whether on campus issues, the war in Indochina, or the issue of Black liberation, the hippies march along with the politicos. Both currents are also cemented by common persecution at the hands of the police. Youth has become Enemy Number 1, to be stopped, searched, arrested and humiliated whenever a cop gets a whim to do so. Minority youth are the first and main victims of police terror, all too frequently the recipients of police bullets, but all young people are its game, particularly those with longer hair.

In recent years anti-imperialist and revolutionary consciousness have grown immensely. There is a greater awareness of who is the enemy and what the ultimate goal of the struggle must be. No longer is this spoken of as some nebulous "participatory democracy," but more and more as socialism. There is a great reading and studying of the writings of revolutionary thinkers, and an increasing number of young people consider themselves "Marxist-Leninists."

A number of factors have led to this growth in anti-imperialist and revolutionary consciousness: First, the turn in the Black liberation struggle from a reformist civil rights outlook to a revolutionary one; second, the impact and lesson of the Cuban

Revolution; and third, the meaning of the Vietnam War and the lessons of the fight against it and of the Vietnamese people's struggle for national liberation.

Both currents of the new radicalism now speak of the need to overthrow the entire imperialist system as the only way to put an end to oppression at home and abroad. Revolution has become the byword. It is on the lips of everyone in the movement; all want it, see it as the only answer, yet few agree on what this really means, how it is to come about, what revolutionaries must do to help "make" the revolution, and what the revolution itself is meant to achieve.

Breaking with reformist illusions marked a most important turning point for the new radicalism. But the failure fully to comprehend what it takes to make a revolution, and what kind of revolution is needed in the first place, has had certain negative effects, creating a crisis of ideology within the movement. Revolutionary rhetoric has become a substitute for strategy and tactics and a cover-up for frustrations and failures.

The policies of the "New Left" have swung from extreme to extreme. Each swing has corrected one set of errors by replacing it with another. Each new tactic chosen is defended by those who favor it as the very alpha and omega of revolutionary principle itself—and God help those who disagree. It is as if the needle of a compass became demagnetized and erratically jumped from side to side, but each direction pointed to was accepted as the true North Pole.

Not so long ago—yet it seems like ages—nonviolence was the great cult and principle. Today some people are making a cult of the opposite view. Ten years ago integration was the cult; for some today it is separation. In the early Sixties right-to-vote legislation and voter registration drives were the be-all and end-all to the winning of freedom, especially in the South. Today there is a cult that frowns on every form of electoral activity, no matter where, when, or for what purpose. In the early years of the new radicalism there was a cult that denigrated the role of leadership and structured organization and countered these with the slogan: "Let the people decide." Now we witness certain small elitist groups making a cult out of their lack of confidence in the ability of the people to decide anything, whether now or in the future, and who view their own self-anointed roles to be as substitutes for the people.

Much of the floundering and confusion within the movement arises from the existence within it of the two currents previously mentioned and their tendency to interpenetrate each other. Ideologically speaking, the tension is between those who begin to see the struggle in Marxist class terms and those who view it in anarchist, individualistic terms. How this conflict is resolved will tell the story—whether the new radicalism will have lasting impact in helping to build a conscious revolutionary Left capable of surviving, and in time winning, against whatever may be thrown at it; or whether it will be broken up and scattered in demoralization and disarray by a ruling class cleverly adept at turning anarchist tendencies within the movement to its own advantage.

What complicates matters, as we have already noted, is that the two tendencies coexist, react upon each other, and produce a weird ideological hodgepodge. It is further complicated because the working class is not yet making its weight felt as the decisive force it must be if revolutionary change is to be.

This last point cannot be overstressed. The great working-class struggles of the Thirties provided the magnet that pulled intellectual youth to the radical orbit, giving them inspiration and perspective. But the relative dormancy of the working-class movement in the postwar period, the venality and corruption of labor leadership, had an opposite effect on radical youth. During the whole first half of the Sixties these youth did try to link up with other opposition currents and movements. They worked valiantly and heroically in the Southern civil rights movement. They tried to organize in the Northern ghettos. Here and there they threw their support to militant labor struggles and sought ties with more progressive labor forces. But these were ephemeral. The most telling blow of all was when they were told by Black leadership—with justice—that their task was to fight against racism and to help organize whites, not Blacks. Not knowing how to communicate with ordinary white working people, influenced by their own middle-class prejudices against workers, the new radicals began to turn in on themselves. As a consequence the tendency toward anarchistic individualism assumed the ascendancy at the same time that the movement took a leap in revolutionary consciousness.

Under such circumstances, the gap between what one knows should be done and what can be accomplished at the moment is so great that frustrations are more or less inevitable. This is particularly so when there is a total lack of perspective, when the time element is reduced to the immediate moment, when there is no confidence that a mass movement of working people can be built, and when the dire alternatives seem to be either to "drop out," or to seek martyrdom in some form of "revolutionary suicide." Inevitable under such conditions is a proliferation of impetuous, half-baked and scatterbrained schemes, each more fantastic than the other, even though many may be well intentioned.

With times so different it is apparent that forms and methods of struggle must also vary and cannot mechanically repeat former patterns. But these cannot be "invented"; they must arise from life and experience. The difficulty lies in determining which have real substance and which are but artifice.

No one can justifiably claim to have *all* the answers to the problems we face. The world and the times are too different and no easy-cook recipes exist for the baking of tomorrow's cake. Yet it is our contention that the answers can be found only within the framework of Marxism-Leninism, seen as a living, creative, expanding social science. They cannot be found along the anarchist path, for this would only lead the new radicalism into a dismal blind alley.

There can be no insurance against mistakes. Those who choose to do nothing to change the world commit no mistakes; they commit a crime. But what should concern us is not immunity from mistakes, but to find the general *direction* in which the movement must go. If this is sound, mistakes can be corrected; if it is unsound, mistakes become hopelessly compounded.

The youth revolt in its many-sided aspects has been of great and positive value. It has helped to radicalize hundreds of thousands of young people and has challenged the system on its most sensitive and vulnerable side: its moral and ethical hypocrisy. Thus it has weakened the very moral authority upon which the system depends for its so-called consensus rule.

The new radicalism has made important contributions to a better grasp of some of the new features of postwar capitalist society. But it has also spun false theories reflecting a subjective reaction to the specific conditions of the time, seeing these not as temporary and fluid, but as fixed and frozen. It is these false theories that have taken on a life of their own and have now become a major obstacle to the further advance of the movement, particularly at a moment when all signs point to a new period of mounting class struggle ahead. It is to discuss and combat these false theories that this book is written.

CHAPTER II

MAN AND SOCIETY

1. Where Marxism and Anarchism Disagree

MARXISM and anarchism have this in common: Both claim a deep concern for the fate of man and a firm belief in the possibility of a society in which, in the words of the *Communist Manifesto,* "the free development of each is the condition for the free development of all" (p. 31).

Where they part company is in their understanding of the nature of man and society, their estimate of the crisis that grips society, and their approach to its solution.

Anarchism starts its analysis of this crisis with the plight of the individual—abused, oppressed, crushed by the juggernaut of centralized bureaucratic power.

Marxism starts its analysis with society and its division into conflicting classes, exploiting and exploited, as the *root* cause of all oppression and the reason why no man is truly free. Freedom in class society can only be a freedom deformed and conditioned by the interests of the dominant class.

Anarchists believe that the emancipation of the individual comes prior to and is the precondition for the emancipation of the mass. Marxism stresses that the emancipation of the mass from capitalist exploitation and oppression is the precondition for the freedom of the individual.

While most anarchists favor some form of socialist society, many of them believe that the revolutionary transformation from capitalism to socialism has no positive bearing on personal freedom unless it is simultaneously accompanied by the abolition of all forms of State power. Marxists hold that working-class State power is necessary for a considerable time after the revolution in order to hold down the old exploiting classes and prepare the way for a completely classless society. They believe that while the socialist revolution does not solve all the problems of personal freedom, it is the indispensable prerequisite for its fullest attainment.

Logically flowing from their analysis, most anarchists stress the role of the individual and individual action as the key to liberation and to the revolutionary transformation of society. On the basis of its analysis, Marxism emphasizes that the role of the individual can be great to the extent that one understands the class nature of society and places oneself at the service of the conscious united action of the masses.

Anarchism tends to view the revolution as a single act; Marxism, as a prolonged historic period of bitter class struggle, requiring strategy, leadership, organization, coordination of effort, discipline, and immediate as well as ultimate objectives.

Seeing the interests of the individual as being in conflict with those of civil society, anarchism tends to regard all social authority as The Enemy. Marxism, however, holds that there can be no society without some forms of authority. What it seeks to end is *oppressive* authority. Toward that end the immediate enemy is capitalism and its State power.

What appears as new in anarchism is in reality very old; what is old often masquerades as new and as being justified by new times. As times and conditions often change radically, it is more difficult for a new generation, searching for its own answers, to discern the old posing as the new.

Anarchism has had more lives than the proverbial cat. It is as old as resistance to oppression and as young as the hippies and the Weathermen. It has been a recurring phenomenon arising in periods of sharp social tension and crisis, particularly at times when rapid technological change radically alters people's lives and the way they earn their living, eroding their former sense of class cohesion and stability.

It is therefore the viewpoint of marginal social strata from among the middle classes or declassed portions of the population, or of those being violently propelled from one class to another, finding themselves in transition. It is met most frequently among the intellectuals. This has been particularly so in recent times.

Irving L. Horowitz, in the introduction to his anthology of anarchist writings, *The Anarchists,* refers to this tendency. He points to the great increase in the intellectual stratum of society in response to the growing social need for expertise and exact knowledge. But this grouping, he believes, has been "the most defeated victim of over-development." "Knowledge," he points out, "has been effectively separated from power," and is one of the factors contributing to the intellectual's feeling of frustration. "The man of knowledge has been 'on tap' but rarely 'on top'" (p. 27).

Lenin too dealt with this phenomenon, already evident in his day. His analysis is deeper, more profound, and shows the class roots of the problem. In an article written at the end of 1899 as a review of a book written by Karl Kautsky, Lenin wrote:

Inall spheres of people's labour, capitalism increases the number of *office and professional workers* with particular rapidity and makes a growing demand for intellectuals. The latter occupy a special position among the other classes, attaching themselves partly to the bourgeoisie by their connections, their outlooks, etc., and partly to the wage-workers as capitalism increasingly deprives the intellectual of his independent position, converts him into a hired worker and threatens to lower his standard of living. The transitory, unstable, contradictory position of this stratum of society now under discussion is reflected in the particularly widespread diffusion in its midst of hybrid, eclectic views, a farago of contrasting principles and ideas, an urge to rise verbally to the higher spheres and to conceal the conflicts between the historical groups of the population with phrases—all of which Marx lashed with his sarcasm half a century ago ("A Review of Kautsky's Book" p. 202).

If this was true at the turn of the century, it is doubly so today. The parasitism of the system has grown to monstrous proportions. The signs of rot and decay, of the wholesale wastage and destruction of human and material resources, are all about us. Under these conditions it is not surprising that intellectual youth, separated as they have been in such large numbers from any form of useful, productive labor, and revolting against the petty-bourgeois philistine atmosphere that blankets the country, should become prone to anarchist individualist trends.

2. Anarchism: Its Many Faces

IT WOULD be a mistake to view anarchism as a cloth woven from only one strand. Horowitz identifies eight distinct, yet intertwining cords, among which are utopian-anarchists, anarcho-syndicalists, anarcho-pacifists, conspiratorial-anarchists, and so forth. Yet despite its many different hues and varying tactics, anarchism represents essentially the same phenomenon—the anguished cry of the individual, outraged, bewildered, frustrated, in face of the immovable monolith of established power and authority.

Anarchism believes that each man must be completely free of external pressures and must be able to make up his own mind as to what is right and what is wrong. It therefore is unalterably opposed to all forms of State power and its laws and institutions. It is as hostile to majority rule as it is to minority rule. A majority can be just as oppressive to a minority as a minority to a majority.*

Anarchists condemn governments for enforcing their rule by the use of armed force, and for resolving disputes between sovereign states by military means, whether through war or coercion. They do not all, however, abhor violence as evil. Some do, and view all who use it as tainted thereby, while others justify individual acts of terror. They reason that since the State lives by the sword it must perish by the sword. They also believe that individual acts of terror are morally justified because they are "propaganda of the deed" that helps to excite and arouse the mass from its lethargy, or to cripple the State machinery, rendering it inoperative. Thus there are anarchists who make a principle of nonviolence, as did Gandhi and Tolstoy, and those who make a principle of violence, as did Bakunin and Most.

*"A man who unconditionally promises in advance to submit to laws that are made or will be made by men, by this very promise renounces Christianity" (Tolstoy, p. 54).

"The anarchist rejects any rule and any person or institution that endeavors to enforce it, because rules endeavor to restrict an individual's freedom. He must also then reject government and the laws that government make. . . . For him no government, no matter how liberal it may be, or how democratic its institutions are, is acceptable" (Jacker, p. 1).

Believing that the evil in men is the product of society held
together by the force of the modern State, anarchists frequently
worship "natural" man and primitive society, as against industrial
man and modern society. They see large-scale industry and
advanced technology as destructive of man's natural aptitudes
and attributes.* Thus there are anarchists who have favored a
return to nature and to small, more primitive, farm and handicraft
modes of life. In this idolatry of the primitive as representative
of the good, the honest and the moral life, there is also a tendency
to identify with the myths and mysticism of more ancient
cultures. To regain the lost past and its imagined peace and
tranquility, anarchists have at times tried to build their own
utopian societies as counter-communities of drop outs from the
world at large.†

This tendency can be traced all the way back to the monastic
settlements of pre-Christian and early Christian religious sects. In
revulsion at the "money changers" who had occupied and defiled
the Temple, at the omnipotent power of the imperial Roman
State, and at the bitter exploitation and oppression of the slave
system, these communities sought to prove by moral example the
superiority of a society based on love instead of greed. They were

*"Ironically, it is the American young, with their underdeveloped radical back-
ground, who seem to have grasped most clearly the fact that, while such
immediate emergencies as the Vietnam War, racial injustice, and hard-core
poverty demand a deal of old-style politicking, the paramount struggle of our day
is against a far more formidable, because less obvious, opponent, to which I will
give the name of 'the technocracy'—a social form more highly developed in
America than in any other society" (Roszak, p. 51).

"It is indeed our industrial way of life that lends sanction to militarism and
colonialism. Our enemy . . . is the Standard of Living . . . our greatest need to
disassociate ourselves from the industrial-scientific madness that rules our lives"
(Shapiro).

†"*Gary Snyder:* 'Well, this is what I've been telling kids all over Michigan and
Kansas. . . . I say, okey, get in touch with the Indian culture here. Find out what
was here before. Find out what the mythologies were. Find out what the local
deities were. . . . Then decide how you want to make your living here. Do you
want to be a farmer, or do you want to be a hunter and food gatherer?'

"*Timothy Leary:* 'Gary, that's one of the wisest things I've heard anyone say in
years. Exactly how it should be done'" ("Interview," *San Francisco Oracle,*
February 1967).

organized along communistic lines; all possessions were owned in common and all material things shared equally. But it was a utopian and ascetic form of communism, a communism of distribution but not yet of production, and a communism outside of society, against the larger society. As a consequence, the only thing it could distribute equally was scarcity. The productive forces of society were still too feebly developed to meet the needs of all. This was even less possible in tiny, isolated colonies, separated from the material resources, the increasing knowledge, and the greater division of labor of the outside world.

These communal societies were therefore doomed to failure despite their high moral quality. A combination of internal disillusion and dissension, and external pressures, led to their downfall. These difficulties arose from the inability to compete with, or to escape the influence of, the world around them.* Unable to build utopian islands on earth they began to build them in heaven. Religious superstition was the opiate that made the hell of earth more endurable, just as Zen Buddhism, rock music and pot have become the opiates that enable many youth today to escape to the new found heaven and haven of the "Woodstock Nation."

Utopian societies were also built in the early capitalist era. A number of the most important of these were planted on United States soil by migrants from Europe or under the influence of European Utopian Socialists like Robert Owen and Charles Fourier. They arose as reactions to the deleterious effects of the Great Industrial Revolution beginning in the 18th century, especially in the country of its birth, Great Britain. Driven from the land in droves to make room for sheep, and into the factories by the lash of hunger and the club of vagrancy laws, the early factory workers resorted to acts of violence directed against the

---

*"They never dreamed that if men were offered the truth they would not leap for it, that if they were told ugly facts they would prefer pleasant lies, that if reasonable ideals were offered them they would continue to act as their fathers had done; they did not see that the follies of the past were not only imposed but ingrained, that men carried their history not only on their backs but in their heads" (Martin, p. 191).

machine, while some sought escape in religious mysticism and here and there in utopian societies.

It soon became clear that industrial society was here to stay and that there was no escape from it. The former peasants and their urban-born sons and daughters had to adjust to their new working-class status and to enter into struggle against their new capitalist barons.

A new form of anarchism, modified by this working-class experience, then arose in the late 19th century, especially in Spain, France, Italy, but also in the United States. Anarcho-syndicalism recognized the need for trade union struggle and even accepted socialism as a goal. But its concept of the new society and how to achieve it was warped by the anarchist mold in which it was shaped. It advocated that the workers in each plant take it over and become its owners by the means of one great general strike. Then the syndicalist factory bodies would organize the free exchange of their products and this would constitute the new anarcho-syndicalist socialist system. This concept made no room for political organization or political struggle. It did not indicate what should be done about the repressive bourgeois State machine and, assuming it was to be overthrown, what would replace it.

The anarchist believes that the salvation of mankind lies in each human being taking his stand against all forms of social authority. Only in this way can the evil of civil society be fought, the State subverted by civil disobedience, each person enabled to gain personal freedom, and the path opened for the emancipation of humanity.

The necessity for individual participation, for individual direct action, is a moral imperative for anarchism. Action may not bring tangible results, but it does bring "personal redemption." "The revolutionary deed is useful *in its nature,* over and above political success or failure, precisely because action with a moral purpose is redemptive" (Horowitz, p. 56).

The revolution starts with individuals remaking themselves, changing their life styles, providing moral example to others.

.

Thus anarchism preaches the "propaganda of the deed" as the most important thing of all. Each person must be an activist, must "do his own thing," for this is far more important than acting in accord with social theories, strategies, or concrete programs for social change.

With the stress being placed on each individual doing his own thing, it is quite evident that organizational discipline and coordinated mass action become extremely difficult to attain. Matters of policy within the movement have no way of being resolved, for even when consensus is achieved there is no way of enforcing it and no feeling of responsibility for upholding it.

Every organization and movement requires some kind of structure and leadership. These in turn create problems of egoism, selfishness and bureaucratic practices. Thus anarchists tend to frown on structured organizations and strong leadership.* Just as the least government is presumed to be the best government, so the least organization and leadership are presumed to be the best organization and leadership. And if the tactics and methods of certain individuals prove highly injurious to the common cause, no one can say them nay. In the first place, there frequently is no recognition of a "common" cause. Then, if the real revolution consists in each person doing his own thing, how can anyone argue that the interests of the revolution demand that he not do his thing! And under such circumstances who can distinguish between sincere, mistaken ways of doing things and the quite deliberate harmful acts of the agent provocateur?

No wonder someone once remarked in jest that what's wrong with the anarchists is that they just can't get themselves organized.

The above general remarks about anarchist beliefs, like all generalizations, is a shoe that fits no particular foot. For example, in showing the anarchist disdain for structured organization and discipline, we are well aware that the conspiratorial school of anarchism demands the very tightest organization. Yet this is not

---

*"There are no Digger leaders. Only Spokesmen. . . . The Digger *modus operandi* is 'do your thing'" (Gleason).

a challenge to its basic premises, only a specific approach to applying them. It is still motivated by the notion that everything depends upon the single heroic individual or small elite handful who must force the masses into a showdown or, should this be impossible, replace them itself.

3. Anarchism as a Reaction to Power

WHAT COMPLICATES a discussion of anarchism and confuses many people is that some of its general observations have validity. The problem to which it addresses itself is real. We have said that the first concern of anarchism is with the fate of the individual in the face of omnipotent power. No one can deny that the centralization and magnification of power is greater, more immense, more all-pervading today than at any other time in history. From competitive, free-enterprise, small-scale capitalism, the country has traveled to large-scale, trustified, monopoly capitalism with its gargantuan industrial conglomerates and multi-national corporations.

The computer has also entered our lives to tabulate, register, cross-file and index more facts about each of us than we could possibly know ourselves. And the revolution in electronics enables authority to look, listen, tape and record every conversation and happening in our daily lives, no matter how private, should it have the whim to do so—and, unfortunately, it frequently does.*

---

*"Counting other kinds of semi-automated records—mechanical card indexes and information on microfilm, for example—the Government, alone, already has various kinds of sensitive information on about 50 million people. The number and variety grows daily" (*New York Times*, December 27, 1970).

The Senate Subcommittee on Constitutional Rights "has already discovered that the Civil Service Commission keeps a total of more than 15 million names in a 'security' file; that thousands of other names are being taped into the computerized files of the Justice Department's Civil Disturbance Group; that a computer at the Secret Service can print out a list of all the left-leaning or peace activists in, say, Madison, Wisc., with moles on their right cheek; and that the Department of Transportation has an electronic dossier of all 2.6 million Americans who have ever had a driver's license suspended or revoked in any state in the country" (*Ibid.*).

The auto has taken over the streets of our cities and a new generation of cliff dwellers may soon forget that flowers, plants and trees are living, growing organic forms of life, giving off a delicate fragrance and not lifeless, plastic imitations. And it has even been suggested that plastic flowers have their advantages— they neither wilt nor need water. No wonder we have had a generation of flower children.

Nor should we be surprised when young people go off on their own to commune with, or should we say commiserate with nature, and to make artistic things with their own hands, objecting to everything being machine punch-pressed, including their lives.

As for the government, when was it more removed from the people? This is government of, by, and for the ultra-rich. What real meaning have elections, when it takes vast sums in the millions of dollars to participate in them, let alone try seriously to win them? Only when a section of the ruling class has its own particular stake in the election outcome, can a somewhat "better" candidate win out against a "worse" one. Lyndon Johnson's brother recently admitted something everyone really knows but is nonetheless worth repeating: "When a candidate has to raise hundreds of dollars, sometimes many thousands from a single fat cat, can anyone seriously believe those big contributors are merely interested in good government?" (Sam Houston Johnson, *New York Post*, February 4, 1970). Who seriously believes they are interested in good government at all? And good government for whom?

Anarchism in the past found its most fertile soil in countries with autocratic rule. Monarchist Spain, Italy and tsarist Russia had long spells of anarchist activities. In tsarist Russia anarchism expressed itself in the Tolstoy pacifist version, the Narodnik populist variety, and the Bakunin terrorist kind.

When it is remembered that Washington today is the general-staff headquarters for the world's most powerful imperial nation; when we note the present-day merger between the State apparatus and the industrial-military power; when we stop to think about institutions like the Pentagon, the CIA and the FBI, and the purposes they serve both at home and abroad; when war crime has become our most profitable business and our most dangerous, mad murderers are the respectable men who own our banks, insurance companies and corporations and who run our government, what better can we expect from the local police, and what kind of respect can a young generation have for established authority?

Anarchism, as Lenin pointed out, has often been "a sort of punishment for the opportunist sins of the working class. Both monstrosities mutually supplemented each other" (*"Left-Wing" Communism,* p. 18). This has been certainly true of the United States. The wave of anarchism that spread through the ranks of super-exploited immigrant workers in the United States in the 1870s and 1880s, was a reaction, in part at least, to the opportunism that had engulfed the National Labor Union and the Socialist Labor Party of that period (*See* Foster, 1952, p. 66). Likewise the anarcho-syndicalism of the Wobbly (IWW) period of the pre-World War I decade was a militant rejoinder to the sell-out, class-collaboration policies of the Gompers-led AFL leadership (*See* Foster, 1952, p. 111).

But there has never been a more shameful period of labor-leadership betrayal of the working man and the people than is the case today. Having joined with the employers and government to drive the Left, particularly the Communists, out of the labor movement during the Cold War hysteria of the Fifties, the great majority of labor leaders have made their peace with the system. Most of them have been shamefully silent about the Vietnam War or loud in its support. With the exception of an honorable few, most of the labor leaders have done little if anything to make the war an issue of discussion and action inside the ranks of the labor movement. Only one or two labor leaders has thus far had the courage to challenge Meany on the floor of an AFL convention. And most union leaderships have also played the game of big business by closing their eyes to, or cooperating with, the way in which the large corporations use the pretext of wage increases to hike prices and profits.

What about the liberals? What role have they played? Now that the Sixties have vanished in the Valhalla of departed decades, it is hard to believe, after what we now know, how far off our most renowned, learned and respected liberal soothsayers have been in their estimate of the times.

Gazing into their crystal balls, the liberal spokesmen of the Fifties saw the Sixties as the decade of such general well-being and peace that it would bear out their contention that "the end of ideology" had come. Of course, they never meant the end of all ideology, only that of vital dissent: of radical, revolutionary and socialist thought. It seemed to liberalism that the old rapacious capitalism had been transformed into a young, benevolent "People's Capitalism." Even prizes were offered to find a better name for the emotive word, for after all capitalism was no longer really capitalism.*

Is it any wonder that the young cats of the new generation have such contempt for liberalism as an ideology and a way of life?

The "Old Left" also shares some of the responsibility for the drift of so many young people to anarchist ways of thinking. The conditions produced by postwar developments were so different from the prewar situation that communication between the generations would have been difficult under the best of circumstances. The older generation of the Thirties and early Forties had confronted two main problems—a ravaging ten-year-long economic crisis and the rise of fascism as a world force. Haunted by both of these experiences, the older Left generation tended to read the future somewhat mechanically from the scrolls of the past. This does not mean that economic crisis and fascism are now *passé*. By no means! But it is true, nonetheless, that the

---

*Here are two typical examples of the thinking of the time:

"Today these old sweeping issues have largely disappeared. The central domestic problems of our time are more subtle and less simple. They relate not to basic clashes of philosophy or ideology, but to ways and means of reaching common goals" (Kennedy, 1962).

"This change in Western political life reflects the fact that the fundamental problems of the industrial revolution have been solved. . . . This very triumph of the democratic social revolution in the West ends domestic politics for those intellectuals who must have ideologies or utopias to motivate them to political action" (Lipset, p. XXI).

postwar quarter of a century has not witnessed a deep-going economic crisis such as the capitalist world went through in the Thirties. Moreover, the postwar forms of rule in the United States and in most other capitalist countries have been characterized more by a monopoly-imposed type of liberal reactionism than by fascism.

The revolt of the young arose out of the *new* conditions of capitalist rule and was pitted against them. The growing irrationality of the system, the role of militarism and war and of the university in relation to these, the existence of dire poverty as the other side of vulgar affluence, the new forms of imperialist domination over subject peoples abroad and at home, and especially the seeming acquiescence of the adult generation and the great majority of the working class to this situation, are some of the factors that triggered the revolt and influenced its style and direction.

The "Old Left" generation of the Thirties had experienced a great awakening of the working class and the consequent majestic class battles of that period after years of slumber. The young generation has had no such experience. It saw the working class as affected by a period of relative prosperity and had neither the theoretical grounding nor practical experience from which to judge this as a temporary and passing phenomenon. The older generation, on the other hand, while correctly stressing the ultimate decisive role of the working class, frequently tended to underestimate what it would take to pry loose the paralyzing grip of a venal and corrupt labor leadership. Nor did it fully appreciate the role that students and intellectuals could play, given revolutionary understanding, in stirring things up as prelude to a new upsurge of the working class itself.

CHAPTER III

FREEDOM AND SOCIETY

1. The Question of Authority

THE DIVISION between Marxism and anarchism is not over a greater or lesser concern for man, the individual. It is over *how* the individual is to achieve the conditions needed for his fullest development and greatest personal freedom.

Freedom is not and cannot be absolute. It never has been and never will be. It is always limited by the bounds of necessity. These are not only social, as some anarchists seem to think, but also natural.

The laws of nature are in many ways more authoritarian than those of man. In order to live, one must eat; not just anything, only that which the human digestive system can absorb. The man who successfully trained his horse to live without eating soon learned that nature's penalty for violating its laws is severe.

Nor is natural man free to fly like the birds, or free of pestilence and disease, or of the cruel authoritarianism of the elements. He cannot walk naked at the icy polar extremes or wear fur at the equator. And he must strictly obey the law of gravity—whether he knows what it is or not—or pay the full penalty for his folly.

Only with the development of science is man able to "defy" the laws of nature, and even then only within limits. Nature has its own way of extracting both respect and retribution from those who ignore its laws, as we are learning to our sorrow in our own day. We are now paying—and will most likely pay a great deal more—for the careless, senseless befouling of the atmosphere, the pollution of waters, the wastage of natural resources, the overuse and misuse of chemical insecticides, and the general upsetting of the delicate balance between man and his natural environment.

Frederick Engels, in his book *Dialectics of Nature,* discusses this problem. He shows that there are limits even to man's scientific foresight, for it is impossible to foresee *all* the longer-range consequences of present-day actions. That is why the expansion of man's knowledge is a never ending process. Engels gives a simple example. In the mountainous regions of Greece, Spain, etc., where pasture lands are poor and scarce, men substituted the goat for the cow because goats thrive on shrubs and roots as well as grass. They did not foresee that the young growth would all be eaten and in time the forests denuded.

Man's first use of tools, his study of the seasons and the way living things grow; in short, the first slight development of scientific knowledge, made it possible for him to take his greatest leap forward. He was no longer limited to poaching *from* nature, as do all animals, but able to consciously *add* to nature's fertility. With the first development of agriculture and animal husbandry, man was able to *produce,* to *plan*—even if only in a rudimentary fashion—and to create a first surplus over bare sustenance needs.

This great "victory" over nature, this ability to "make" nature give up more of its treasure, was not without a price, its negative side. Early man could only face the vicissitudes of nature by working and living collectively in communal fashion. But with man's ability to produce a surplus, it became possible for some men, by taking possession of land, cattle, tools and property—the means of production—to live in luxury on other men's toil.

To maintain the dominance of master over slave, lord over serf and capitalist over worker; in other words, to defend the interests of the exploiting classes in the various stages of human society since primitive times, repressive institutions became necessary. With the division of society into conflicting economic classes the State was born.

Thus, to the degree that man was successful in his struggle to "control" the forces of nature, he was unsuccessful in preventing the class struggle within society from becoming uncontrollable. What the rapacious jungle beast had been to primitive man, civilized man became to his fellow man. Seeking the moral right to exploit and oppress, the ruling classes proclaimed this right to be the basic law of both nature and society. The struggle of animal species for survival in nature was seen as justification for the struggle between classes of humans in the jungle of society. Yet there is no species other than man that systematically kills its own kind.

It is this regressive side to the great progressive advance of science that is the basis for the anarchist rejection of technological society and all forms of social authority. While it is true that class society did bring with it oppressive authority over people, not all social authority is oppressive. To live in society—and people cannot live without it—each person must accept limits on his or her own freedom of action to the degree that it impinges on the rights and freedom of others. We are not referring to repressive forms of authority imposed to defend vested property rights, but to the natural forms of authority required by any kind of social organization.

No two people can live together, even when they think they can live on love alone, without "sacrificing" a bit of their own personal freedom to do what they please, when they please and how they please. But whatever freedom is lost in one direction is more than gained in another, for two can do what one cannot, and this refers to more than making love. It is impossible to ride in a train or plane, to work in a factory or operate a computer, without accepting or exercising some form of authority.

The anarchist worships more primitive forms of social organization for he believes he can escape from authority. It is true, of course, that the more complex the technology the more need there is for authority. But even in primitive society, in the face of natural disasters like forest fires, droughts or famines, where tight discipline is required for survival, authority to make decisions must be vested in certain individuals; and even if authority is delegated, it is still authority. In hunting and fishing societies where these activities are performed on a group basis, coordination and discipline are essential, as is the power of decision vested in specific individuals. One does not have the freedom to shoot at an approaching herd before it is within range, or to shout and do what would frighten the game away, or to start hoisting the fishing net before the signal to do so is given, and so on.

In early agricultural tribal societies it was the witch doctor, in the name of magic, who decided the time for planting. Even the music and the chanting and dancing in tribal societies served the useful purpose of instilling courage and confidence by frightening the evil spirits away and by rehearsing the hunters or warriors and teaching the children what each had to do when the time for action came. And when certain anti-social acts endangered tribal life, superstitious taboos were employed to enforce compliance.

Thus, only the final authority of death can free humanity from the natural and social forms of authority that come with living.

2. "Do Your Thing!"

IT MAY come as a surprise to some of today's young radicals that when they shout, "Do Your Thing!", this slogan is not as revolutionary and anti-bourgeois as they may think. In reality it is nothing more than psuedo-leftist rhetoric for the ideology that is typically and classically bourgeois.

The burgher of feudal times, the forerunner of the later day capitalist, raised the cry of individual freedom to the top place in his lexicon of bourgeois slogans. He, too, demanded the right to do his own thing without restrictions of any kind. This is what he meant by the watchword, liberty. And while he tried to pass this off as freedom for all of society, he really meant something quite different: The freedom to produce what and how he wanted; the freedom to compete equally with other entrepeneurs in the national market place; the freedom to remove all feudal and monarchical taxes and fetters on production and trade; the freedom to erect a State power that would protect his property interests and that of his class; the freedom to purchase labor power for as little as possible, and the freedom to discard it, like other waste matter, when it no longer was profitable to employ it. And, of course, he also championed "free labor," meaning by this the freedom of the laborer to sell his work ability to an employer for whatever he could get, and the freedom to starve when he did not do so.

We are well aware, of course, that Jerry Rubin and Abbie Hoffman and others who think like them do not mean this kind of bourgeois freedom. But what kind of individual freedom can there be in a class society that does not turn out to be anti-freedom for someone else?

The freedom not to work can be enjoyed—and is being enjoyed to the full—by many of the bourgeoisie. It is a freedom the bourgeoisie can well afford, even when it does not avail itself of it. But what about those who do not have the means for doing so? There is today a considerable number of young people who have made a cult out of not working. Working, in their eyes, is to "join the system," to become "integrated," to "cop-out." Not to work is to "live the revolution."

But when we examine this a bit closer, we find that this freedom to "drop out" is by no means universal. It is both class rooted and class motivated. Horowitz, in the book on anarchism previously quoted, notes that the return to "individualistic patterns" (whatever this means) that anarchists advocate, is only accessible "to the most unusual people." This, he points out, does not broaden the equalitarian democratic base of society, but instead creates the base for a new kind of elitism (p. 592).

Paul Goodman, in his book *Like a Conquered Province*, tells us what it is that is "unusual" about the present young crop of elite hippies, although he himself is quite gushy in effusive praise of them. He writes:

We must remember that these are the young of the affluent society, used to a high standard of living and confident that if and when they want to, they can fit in and make good money. Having suffered little pressure of insecurity, they have little psychological need to climb; just as coming from impeccably respectable homes, they feel no disgrace about sitting a few nights in jail. In their confidence they are aristocrats—en masse. At the same time, the affluent standard of living which they grew up with is pretty synthetic and very much of it is useless and phony, and the poverty of the students is not degraded or insecure but decent, natural, and in many ways more comfortable than their parents' standard, especially if they can always corral obvious goodies like hi-fi equipment and motorcycles. Typically they tour Europe on nothing, sleeping under bridges; but if they get really hungry, they can drop in at the American Express . . . . Thus, they are the first generation in America selective of the standard of living; if this attitude became general it would be a disaster for the expanding GNP"(p. 37).

So, as can be seen, the freedom to live this way is by no means open to all, only to the "aristocrats," who can always drop back in "if and when they want to" and "fit in and make good money;" who can always corral expensive "goodies" from daddy, and who can tour Europe "on nothing," "sleep under bridges," but always fall back on a fat American Express money-order if need be.

3. The Psychedelic Revolution

WHAT ABOUT those who are not that fortunate as to be able to sponge off the old man? There is a way for them, too. In an interview between leading spokesmen of this new "counter culture," the following dialogue took place.

Alan Watts: "Gary [Snyder], I think you have something to say here. Because you, to me, are one of the most fantastically capable drop-out people I have ever met. . . . This is the nitty-gritty. There is where it really comes down to in many people's minds. Where's the bread coming from if everybody drops-out?

Gary Snyder: " . . . we used to go around at one or two in the morning around the Safeway and Piggly Wigglies in Berkeley with a shopping bag, and hit the garbage cans out in back."

Watts: "Can you have a wife and children under such circumstances?"

Snyder: "Yes, I think you can, sure."

Watts: "What about when the state forces you to send the child to school?"

Snyder: "You send it to school."

Timothy Leary: "Oh no, c'mon, I don't see that as drop-out at all" ("Interview," *San Francisco Oracle,* February 1967).

Of course, whether the bread comes from pa's bankroll, from garbage cans, from panhandling, or stealing, it is still far from adding up to a "revolutionary life style" that is going to liberate the individual or society. Nor is it really meant to do so. It is a put-on. It is petty-bourgeois slumming. Only those who know full well that they do not have to live this way, and that they *will not live this way tomorrow,* can "enjoy" the luxury of doing so today.

This may be the new-found freedom of the new aristocrats of whom Paul Goodman sings, but it is no freedom at all for the hungry, the downtrodden, the poor, the oppressed, and the great majority of people who must work if they are to eat and who want to send their children to school and to feed them from the horn of plenty and not from the rotting garbage of a Safeway store.

There is nothing even remotely revolutionary in this. It mocks those who do have to sleep under bridges and live in poverty. Above all, it evades the personal responsibility for entering the struggle to *change* the world. There is really no difference between this kind of drop-out and cop-out. One need but listen to the utterings of the prophets of the new counter culture to recognize this.

Writing in the *Evergreen Review (September 1967)* one enthusiast for the psychedelic revolution tells us that more and more young people "are turning away from traditional forms of dissent because they find dissent meaningless." He lauds the philosophy of the Diggers "as accepting the futility of either fighting or joining the system." And how do they know it is futile? A Digger Statement explains: "A perfection of inner self sometimes attainable through LSD-25 or other psychedelics, reveals the failure of all political games" (Gleason).

If fighting the system is futile, and if this great truth is revealed by the hallucinating powers of LSD, what then are the working people caught in the meshes of the system to do about it? Should workers fight exploitation or cop out? Should welfare mothers demand more aid for their families or are they to feed them on a mixture of garbage and LSD? Should black people fight oppression or go to pot? Should people fight against the war or join Timothy Leary's "psychedelic religious movement."

The Digger Statement goes on to put the alternatives as it sees them. It asks: "Do you want to *show* people a groovy way of life, or do you want to *tell them how to live,* and back it up with bottles, bricks, boards and even bullets?"

This is a very revealing posing of the question. We are given the anarchist-utopian choice of getting away from it all via an underground psychedelic trip to groovyland, or the anarchist-terrorist choice of wholesale violence. With only these two options open, the former has all the advantages. It is "groovy," while dissent is "meaningless."

What about another choice? What about *struggle?* What about helping to build a serious revolutionary movement that can change the way people live, and not merely tell them how to live?

Timothy Leary preaches the same reactionary gospel of passive acceptance of the system in the guise of rejecting it. "Mass movements make no sense to me," he declared in the interview previously mentioned, "and I want no part of mass movements. I think this is the error that the leftist activists are making. . . . I think they should be sanctified, drop out, find their own center, turn on, and above all avoid mass movements, mass leadership, mass followers. I see that there is a great difference—I say incompatible difference—between the leftist activist movement and the psychedelic religious movement."

A bit further on in the dialogue, Allen Ginsberg asks Leary:

Precisely what do you mean by dropping out? . . . For instance, you haven't dropped out, Tim. You haven't dropped out of being a financial promoter of Millbrook, and you haven't dropped out of planning and conducting community organization and participating in it.

And that community organization is related to the national community, too. Either through the Supreme Court, or through the very existence of the dollar that is exchanged for you to pay your lawyers, or to take money to pay your lawyers in the theater. So you can't drop out, like *drop-out*, 'cause you haven't.

Ginsberg knew whereof he spoke. Before the discussion was over Leary casually admitted that, "In the last four months, I have been making about eight thousand dollars a week." ("Interview," *San Francisco Oracle*, February 1967).

4. Madison Avenue Goes "Counter Culture"

THE TRUTH is that the counter culture that was meant to prevent integration into the system, has been taken over by Madison Avenue and the system's hucksters, lock, stock and barrel, or should we say, hair, beads and clothes. Those who started out in revolt against the conformity of short hair and square clothes have become the victims of their own kind of conformity—and just as slavishly authoritarian—of long hair and odd clothes. Fortunes are being minted in selling mod costumes at mad prices in special boutiques of the hippy culture. Nor can we just pass over the unconscionable profits made on the sale of drugs. But a sophisticated young generation that can dig how the "man" runs the show in square society is often blind to how "he" has also taken it over in hippieland.

Roszak, in his book on the counter culture, admits that "whatever the young have fashioned for themselves has rapidly been rendered grist for the commercial mill and cynically merchandised by assorted hucksters—*including* the new ethos of dissent, a fact that creates an agonizing disorientation for the dissenting young (and their critics) . . . " (p. 27)

In Abbie Hoffman's book, *Revolution for the Hell of It,* he brags about his ability to break through the media any time he wants. The media cannot shut him out; oh no! "We have often been accused of being media-oriented," he writes. "As with all criticism, it is both true and not true. The Mobilization had five times the number of press conferences that we did but we received five times the amount of coverage. The impression that we are media freaks is created by our ability to make news" (p. 186-87).

Jerry Rubin prides himself on the same quality. The more eccentric the dress and behavior, the more assurance there is of breaking the media barrier. As Abbie says, "Just do your thing; the press eats it up. MAKE NEWS" (p. 37).

The problem of getting the truth to the people in a country in which the media are corporate owned and controlled is a serious one. Not only are the TV and radio networks, the mass circulation dailies and the slick magazines owned by the ultra-rich, but without fat advertisements from the giant corporations they could not exist, let alone make fabulous profits.

How come then that these media, owned and controlled by the ruling class, are so gullible as to be taken in by the clownish antics of a few eccentric showmen? Roszak touches on this question but does not answer it. "Dissent, the media has decided," he tells us, "is hot copy. But if anything, the media tend to isolate the weirdest aberrations *and* consequently to attract to the movement many extroverted poseurs" (p. 37).

Yes, this is undoubtedly true. It does not answer, however *why* the media isolate the weirdest aberrations. It is true that the media do go for sensationalism and that when man bites dog it is considered news and not the other way around. But we are dealing with a sophisticated and highly class-conscious control of the news. When something is to be blocked out, it is blocked out, period. And when it cannot be blocked out it is slanted, and with a vengeance. The news of the youth revolt cannot be blocked out. When millions of young people begin to fight the dogs that bite them, this is NEWS in capital letters. But through the conscious exposure of weirdos, the media is slanting this historic development so as to foster the impression that the whole youth revolt is weird, absurd, crazy. In this way many people who realize that there is something wrong with the system are led to believe that there is no real answer to this; that the rebelling young would only make things worse.

Abbie and Jerry think that the media are suckers for their put-ons. Even if they are right, what about the people to whom their message is beamed? Are they to be treated as suckers, too? And who is to tell what is meant as put-on and what is not?

There is still another aspect to this. Constant exposure to the media can be a heady experience and quite corrupting. One begins to think media, act media, and become Peck's bad boy for the media. And before long it is the media that decide what is to be said, for after all they know best what makes the news. Nor is all this without its remuneration. Books are written, laid out and plotted on Madison Avenue, and the more times four letter words are used the greater the lucre.

Nor has the movement any control over its media-picked spokesmen. Anarchism is opposed to leaders for leaders can be bought off, become bureaucrats, etc.* But without organization and leadership nothing can be accomplished. As bad as some organizations may be there is still more chance of exercising control over leaders than in the anarchist world of no organization and no leaders, where media chosen no-leaders gain the right to speak and act as if they were the chosen representatives of the movement, but without restraint or control of any kind.

---

*"To begin with, we are convinced that the revolutionary cannot and must not be a leader" (Cohn-Bendit, p. 262).

CHAPTER IV

THE ROOTS OF INDIVIDUALISM

1. The Crisis of Liberalism

INDIVIDUALISM, WE have said, is the classical ideology of the bourgeoisie. Anarchism is not its opposite pole, only a more radical variant of the same theme. It is therefore particularly attractive to those who, having become disillusioned with the liberal version, seek an alternative to it within the framework of individualism itself.*

This is particularly so in the United States. The roots of individualism are deeply imbedded in the American historical experience and in the nation's psychology and mythology. In many ways the United States has been the most bourgeois-minded of all countries. The notion that all individuals enjoyed equal rights and opportunities was largely a myth even in the heyday of early American capitalism. It was always a strictly limited right and never existed for the Black, Indian or Chicano peoples. Nor have women ever enjoyed full equality with men. Yet early capitalism did consist largely of small producers; there was a greater opportunity for working people (whites) to move up the class ladder; political rule was looser and more decentralized; the standard of living was generally higher than elsewhere; and even though the class struggle periodically assumed extremely sharp and bloody forms, there was nonetheless a certain material foundation for the illusion that freedom was universal. There was

---

*"The philosophy of the anarchists is bourgeois philosophy turned inside out. Their individualistic theories and their individualistic ideal are the very opposite of socialism. Their views express, not the future of bourgeois society, which is striding with irresistible force towards the socialization of labor, but the present and even past of that society, the domination of blind chance over the scattered and isolated small producers" (Lenin, "Socialism and Anarchism," p. 73).

enough flexibility and fluidity in class relations to prop the illusion that success depended largely on a combination of pluck and luck. Thus the vast majority thought in individualist and not in class terms.*

This is still largely the case. Since World War II, there has even been a bolstering of certain illusions. On the surface at least, the nation's economy appears to be a vehicle that has been running without a major breakdown for a quarter of a century. Many of those who starved in the Thirties now think they "have it made." The demands of science and technology for greater knowledge and professional skill have also enabled more workers' sons and daughters to enter the professions than before seemed possible. And the disposition to think in individualist instead of class terms is vividly illustrated by the fact that this is the only developed capitalist country in the world in which a mass working class or labor party, reformist or otherwise, has not arisen.

Yet within this continuity of both tradition and illusion something new is happening. Liberalism, as the classical political expression of individualism, is in deep crisis. The old melody still lingers on, but the song itself has ended. Two developments account for this: First, the unrelenting trend toward an ever greater concentration of economic power and wealth—a tendency inherent in capitalist production relations in which big fish constantly devour smaller ones—stands in glaring and even mocking refutation of the classical liberal *laissez-faire* doctrine. This has been true for a long time. But it is only recently that this inexorable trend has found its reflection in a growing realization—particularly among young people—that there is something fundamentally wrong with the system, and that individual rights, aspirations, and youthful dreams, are being mangled by the wringer of monopoly power. Thus the crisis of the system has

---

*"Of all politically advanced people, the Americans are the only ones who started in an historical golden age of anarchy. Having gotten rid of the king—he was always far away, as well as being only an English king—they were in no hurry to find another sovereign or even reconstruct a concept of sovereignty. For almost 30 years after the outbreak of the Revolution, almost nobody bothered to vote in formal elections (often less than 2 per cent), and the National Constitution was the concern of a few merchants and lawyers" (Goodman, p. 135).

also produced a crisis for liberalism. The political philosophy of the bourgeoisie in the period of rising competitive capitalism, liberalism, ceases to be the dominant capitalist view in the era of its crisis and decay. The needs of economic monopoly soon dictate the need for political monopoly. The needs of political monopoly, in turn, soon dictate the need for political repression. This is what Lenin meant when he said in *Imperialism* that the growth of monopoly produces a tendency toward "reaction all along the *line*." (p. 110).

We have seen this trend at work for years. Despite the continued use of liberal rhetoric, most liberal congressmen, governors or mayors today are reactionary as compared to their counterparts of an earlier era. The confidence of the bourgeoisie of the pre-monopoly era in both itself and its system permitted its *laissez-faire* economic doctrine to be reflected in a *laissez-faire* political climate. This too, of course, was limited by class interests. The ruling class never permitted its rule as such to be challenged. It has been one of the most brutal ruling classes in history in its racist oppression of the Black, Red, Brown and Yellow peoples. Yet all this was done within the suave, self-confident view that American capitalism was truly the best of all societies and deserved eternal life.

The crisis of the system has produced its political counterpart in an extreme-right current that openly challenges liberalism both politically and philosophically. It strives to push liberalism more and more to the Right. At the same time it builds a base for its own more extreme fascist-like solution should that become necessary. Yet it is interesting to note that this more open political reaction, whether of a Wallace, Agnew, Reagan or Buckley, challenges liberalism on its own grounds, that of individualism. It strives demagogically to appear opposed to "big government," "big business," and "big labor." Wallace even promised the voters that he would shift the tax burden to the ultra-rich and would remove the tax exempt status from the billion dollar corporate-controlled foundations. The Right is now the defender—in words—of *laissez-faire* capitalism and speaks in behalf of the "little fellow," the "silent majority," who, apparently, cannot speak for themselves. It blames the crisis of our times not on the capitalist system but on liberal welfare do-goodism, big government spending, and wishy-washy permissiveness. The Conservative Party of New York State, the private political poaching grounds of the Connecticut-based Buckley tribe, even uses as a slogan, "Less government—more individual responsibility!" And writers in Buckley's slick *National Review* refer to themselves as "libertarians."

2. Libertarians of the Right, Left and Center

THIS APPEAL to individualism on the part of the anarchist "Left", the liberal Center, and the reactionary Right, has confused some people. Carl Oglesby is one of them. He wants to discard all old political and class lines and unite the libertarians of the Right, Left and Center into a new great popular alliance. Seeing the issue of individual freedom as central, he believes that this central question "is not clarified, it is obscured, by our common political categories of left, right and center," and that "it is obscured by the traditional American debate about socialism versus capitalism versus the Keynesian mixed economy."

The kind of economic system we have seems to be unimportant to Oglesby because "the socialist radical, the corporatist conservative, and the welfare state liberal are all equally capable of leading forward into the totalized society." In other words, for him the threat to individual freedom comes equally from socialist radicals, corporation conservatives and middle-class liberals—they all can bring on totalitarian repression.

Oglesby sees nothing but disaster ahead if these "new realities are not penetrated and a fundamental ideological rearrangement does not take place." And such a rearrangement is possible, according to him, because the question of individual freedom is "in the grain of the American libertarian right" as it is "in the grain of American democratic populism." The fact that the black liberation and student movements "are called leftist means nothing." They are all part of the great American "libertarian tradition." "In a strong sense, the Old Right and the New Left are morally and politically coordinate" (Oglesby, pp. 164-67).

That Oglesby sees a moral and political affinity between the

"Old Right" and the "New Left" is an indication of how far off he has wandered. His seemingly non-class or above-class Olympian view is in reality the outlook of the petty-bourgeois intellectual seeking some form of accommodation with the system.

There is a real problem, of course, in some of the questions raised by Oglesby, which he has unfortunately obscured by a smorgasbord serving of the Right and Left on a single libertarian platter. The extreme Right has wrapped itself in the flag of individual freedom. It tries to communicate with the average person and to appeal to his sense of justice, while taking advantage of and building upon his prejudices. On the other hand, sections of the new radicalism have an attitude of disdain for the ordinary working man and woman; reject all American tradition, the good with the bad; take a completely nihilist position toward national pride and patriotism, permitting these to be taken over by the pay-triots, the jingoists, the imperialists.

Had Oglesby called attention to these defects he would have performed a worthwhile service. But when he calls for a wiping out of political and class lines, when he postulates the need of an amorphous unity of Right and Left around the abstract question of individual freedom, he is doing a grave disservice to the cause of freedom. He is forgetting what Abe Lincoln said about the wolf and the sheep. To speak of abstract freedom is to forget that freedom for the exploiter is non-freedom for the exploited. Surely the cause of freedom cannot be advanced by concealing the truth that it is the system of monopoly capitalism that encroaches upon freedom and that only the struggle against it can win it for the people.

Once the question of individual freedom is abstracted from class relations, the class struggle and the struggle of oppressed peoples, it becomes a highway with many entrances but no exits. Carl Oglesby, unfortunately does not see the struggle in such terms. He is lost on the highway that leads nowhere.

3. Anarchism as the Reverse Side of Liberalism

THE RULING class has always practiced a clever interlacing of methods of reform with methods of repression. Even the most reactionary government indulges in certain reforms at times and there are always sections of the population who see in liberal reform the solutions to their own particular problems. Hence there is always some material basis for the existence of liberal moods and illusions. Such exist today.

Moreover, liberalism is still needed by monopoly capitalism. It is interesting to note in this respect how many of the so-called liberal foundations, such as Ford, Rockefeller, Carnegie, and others, have been set up, financed and controlled by the largest and most reactionary corporate interests in the country. In an era of great social ferment the ruling class needs a liberal movement that can act as a safety valve for mass discontent and keep masses from moving in a completely independent political direction. Thus, side by side with the greater entrenchment of monopoly domination in the country, the Democratic Party, controlled by the ruling class, has been permitted to take on the guise of a liberal party. While the Labor Party in Great Britain plays the same kind of a liberal role, the ruling class of this country prefers a situation in which no working-class party, not even a reformist kind, can make its appearance.

What is significant about the present period is that liberalism as a *system of beliefs,* as the panacea for what ails the system, is being challenged on a wider front and more basically than ever. This is because liberalism has shown itself to be totally incapable of explaining the crisis of our times. It offers little more than Geritol to meet the iron-blood deficiency of a system whose illness is chronic and, in the long run, terminal.*

---

*"As a compelling, or even a useful, ideology, liberalism belongs to the heroic epoch of the middle classes of the already industrialized nations of capitalism; nowadays, as ideology and as rhetoric, it is much more useful as a defense of the *status quo....*

"To the world's range of enormous problems, liberalism responds with its verbal fetish of 'Freedom', plus a shifting series of opportunistic reactions. The world is hungry; the liberal cries, 'Let us make it free!' The world is tired of war; the liberal cries, 'Let us arm for peace!' The peoples of the world are without land; the liberal cries, 'Let us beg some of the landed oligarchs to parcel some of it out!' In sum: the most grievous charge today against liberalism and its conservative varieties is that they are so utterly *provincial,* and thus so irrelevant to the major problems that must now be confronted in so many areas of the world" (C. Wright Mills, p. 29).

Liberalism and anarchism have the same class roots and represent the same holding tight to petty-bourgeois individualism. Both are also essentially utopian. Liberalism is utopian in its belief that capitalism can be reformed into something other than an oppressive, exploitative society, and anarchism is utopian in its belief that society can be revolutionized without mass struggle, organization, discipline, leadership, and without the winning and the use of State power to crush the resistance of the old exploiting classes.

There is one very important difference between liberalism and anarchism. Liberalism reflects the belief that the system can be patched up by measures of reform, that things can be set right if only men of good will—liberals, of course—are permitted to have their say and their way. It believes that all social problems are amenable to peaceful solution if there is only a willingness on all sides to compromise a little. Liberalism reflects, therefore, the normal middle-class disposition to vacillate, conciliate and to avoid sharp confrontation at all costs.*

Anarchism, as distinct from liberalism, represents a reaction to the failures and hypocrisy of liberalism and is a violent rejoinder to it. It, too, reflects the mood of middle-class individuals, but of those who feel the ground being moved from under them, who no longer have confidence in the normal functioning of the system, and who fly to the other extreme in rage and despair but within the same individualist range. It is a subjective reflection of the growing anarchy and disintegration in society. And these are more visible and more shocking in their traumatic effects in the United States than in any other country. Here the ravages of social decay and disease stand out in even bolder relief because

---

*Two examples come to mind: In a *Life* magazine review of the movie "The Molly Maguires," the producer is applauded for "making this a liberal film in the best sense of that word, fair to both protagonists." Fair, that is, to both the exploited miners and their militant leaders and to the coal operators and their Pinkerton agents!

Former Supreme Court Justice Arthur Goldberg, running for Governor of the State of New York, gave a classical example of the liberal mind at work. He is quoted in the *New York Times* (May 27, 1970) as saying: "Despite the fact that I am a liberal who does not talk out of both sides of my mouth, they [the conservatives] recognize that I am a man who believes in reconciliation." (!)

of the contrast with the gaudy affluence of this richest imperial state on earth.

Lenin had occasion to note this petty-bourgeois propensity to become furious "over the horrors of capitalism." He referred to it as "a social phenomenon which, like anarchism, is characteristic of all capitalist countries." But this mood is far more prevalent today, because the crisis of the system is many times more severe. Every important problem of our day flows out of and in turn feeds back to, the fundamental crisis of the capitalist system itself.

There is reason enough for being furious "over the horrors of capitalism." There is also more reason than ever to heed Lenin's warning that such revolutionism is unstable, barren, and liable "to become swiftly transformed into submission, apathy, fantasy, and even into a 'mad' infatuation with one or another bourgeois 'fad'" (*"Left-Wing" Communism*, p. 17). Proudhon, the father of anarchism, illustrated this to perfection. He leapt from fad to mad fad and ended up as a stark reactionary.

An ideological break with liberalism is indispensable for a truly revolutionary point of view. But anarchism and the psuedo-Left romanticism that resembles it are not that point of view. They represent a nihilist negation of liberalism without any real substitution for it. They tend to make liberalism the single target of attack and fail to distinguish between liberalism as a system of thought and individual liberals with whom it is possible and necessary to unite on one or another issue. Like former sinners now turned evangelists, they tolerate least of all the image of their former selves as reflected in others.

Just as the failures of liberalism feed anarchist moods, so in turn, the failures of anarchism with its total dependence on spontaneity and its rejection of political struggle, leave the masses at the mercy of one or another bourgeois current. For the ruling ideology of any given period is the ideology of its ruling class. Without an ideology that fundamentally challenges the ruling ideology, and shows why and how society can be reconstructed along entirely new and revolutionary lines, the working class cannot develop an independent political perspective, independent class organizations, and is always ready prey for one or another bourgeois fad.

Hence anarchism, which considers itself to be the sworn foe of liberalism, actually induces the people to go back to liberalism. One reason for this is that anarchism, decrying program, organization, mass movements and leadership, makes it easier for liberals to capture and lead the struggles and movements around vital needs, while the psuedo-Leftists stand aloof from them.

Spontaneity must be seen as an indispensable factor of the very greatest significance in every mass struggle and upsurge. No revolutionary movement can succeed without it. The spontaneous anger and action of the masses can arise so suddenly and strike with such elemental fury as to lead to insurrection itself and to the toppling of government. The 1905 and February 1917 Russian Revolutions were such combustible explosions. But without revolutionary theory and leadership, mass spontaneity is helpless to replace the old with something fundamentally new.

In his seminal booklet, *What Is To Be Done?* written in 1901-02, Lenin discusses the question of spontaneity at considerable length. Analyzing the movement as it was developing in tsarist Russia, Lenin shows that the "spontaneous element, in essence, represents nothing more nor less than consciousness in *embryonic* form." Even the primitive revolts that had taken place in earlier decades, he points out, "expressed the awakening of consciousness to a certain extent. The workers were losing their age-long faith in the permanence of the system which oppressed them and began, I shall not say to understand, but to sense the necessity for collective resistance, definitely abandoning their slavish submission to the authorities. But this was, nevertheless, more in the nature of outbursts of desperation and vengeance than of *struggle*."

What Lenin means by struggle he makes clear. "The strikes of the nineties," he adds, "revealed far greater flashes of consciousness; definite demands were advanced, the strike was carefully timed, known cases and instances in other places were discussed, etc. The revolts were simply the resistance of the oppressed, whereas the systematic strikes represented the class struggle in embryo, but only in embryo."

Note how carefully Lenin distinguishes between spontaneous mass outbursts, even revolts, from *organized* forms of struggle. The latter already represent the class struggle, but only in an embryonic form. These strikes "marked the awakening antagonisms between workers and employers; but the workers were not, and could not be, conscious of the irreconcilable antagonism of their interests to the whole of the modern political and social system. . . . In this sense, the strikes of the nineties, despite the enormous progress they represented as compared with the 'revolts', remained a purely spontaneous movement" (p. 31). What was lacking was the consciousness that the struggle must lead to the overthrow of capitalist rule and its replacement with working-class rule and socialism. Without this understanding, wrote Lenin, "The spontaneous working class movement means the ideological enslavement of the workers by the bourgeoisie. . . . Hence our task . . . is to combat spontaneity" (p. 41).

4. Subjectivism and "Gut" Reaction

WHEN THE capitalist class was still a progressive class, the bourgeois system seemed to be the embodiment of human reason. It was the Age of Reason as against the obscurantism of feudal medieval society. There was some justification for this view. Karl Marx and Frederick Engels, the two intellectual and revolutionary giants who laid bare the hollowness of the bourgeois order and scientifically proved its transitory nature, still gave the devil its due. In their monumental *Communist Manifesto,* written more than a century ago, they affirmed that:

The bourgeoisie, during its rule of scarce one hundred years, has created more massive and colossal productive forces than all preceding generations together. Subjection of nature's forces to man, machinery, application of chemistry to industry and agriculture, steam navigation, railways, electric telegraphs, clearing of whole continents for cultivation, canalization of rivers, whole populations conjured out of the ground— what earlier century had even a presentiment that such productive forces slumbered in the lap of social labor? (pp. 13-14).

Now that the capitalist system is a dying one, it is no longer the embodiment of reason. Yet from the viewpoint of liberalism, it is the only rational system. What liberalism cannot see is that its own reason is class based and motivated. It is but an expression of its own middle-class position in between the two major classes of modern society. What it fails to understand is that the failings of the system do not come from lack of reason. From the class viewpoint of the imperialists the aggression against Vietnam was both rational and reasonable. What for them is irrational and unreasonable was the kind of stubborn, heroic and successful resistance put up by the Vietnamese people. Only to the extent that the imperialist aggression is proving to be a disaster for them, do certain groups within the ruling class begin to see the utter irrationality, if not insanity, of their action. But to the extent that they see this at all, it is because the aggression is failing. Were it succeeding they would hail it to the heavens. To see the irrationality of the Vietnam—now Indochina—War in a deeper historic sense requires accepting a revolutionary point of view. It requires recognizing that the continued existence of the imperialist-capitalist system has become irrational, unreasonable and untenable.

In rejecting liberal rationalism, anarchism tends to reject rational thought as such. Like some existentialists, it accuses rational thought of viewing man as object instead of subject, that is, of treating man as something alien and foreign to himself. In this separation of man as subject from man as object we see once again the pitting of man the individual, against man the social being.

Dialectical materialism makes no such separation between humans as subjects and humans as objects. Man is both subject to himself, object to others. He is both an individual and a social being. As men consciously act together they become a subjective force capable of shaping objective developments. But they remain at one and the same time a force *for themselves* and a force *for history,* i.e., an integral part of objective reality.

The separation of man as subject from man as object, and the failure to find a scientific rational explanation for the crisis of our times, leads to a tendency to deny the very existence of objective truth; at least the ability of man to comprehend it. Anarchism believes that each person must be his own judge of right or wrong and is, in the last analysis, only responsible to his own conscience for his acts. Reason is suspect; instincts and feelings are trusted. Subjective intuition, it is believed, comes closer to the truth than reasoning based on the objective study of things. One must act, therefore, in accord with one's innermost "gut" reactions. To get others to act likewise it is necessary to communicate with their emotions over and above their intellect; it is necessary to arouse instinctive responses—dulled and debased by civil society—to come alive again. In this is seen the hope for the future. And toward this end a language is advocated that is highly emotive and speaks to the "gut" and not to the "mind."*

It can readily be seen how slogans like "Do it!", "Do your thing!" fit into such a philosophy. The use of words for their shock value follows from this same line of thinking. This is all part of a new kind of psychological shock-therapy. The more words that produce emotional response the better. Whether the response is favorable or unfavorable is immaterial.†

Words of course are weapons and people use them and react to them both intellectually and emotionally. A person who reacts against injustice only intellectually, who does not passionately hate oppression and exploitation and does not use strong language to convey this feeling, is not a human being of flesh and blood, but a programmed computerized brain, a machine. However if one pits instinct and emotions against, or places them

---

*The French anarchist, Daniel Guérin, writes that "Anarchism can be described first and foremost as a visceral revolt" (p. 13).

†Jerry Rubin: "You know why he [Dave Dellinger] got jailed? Because he expressed emotion. That's what an obscene word is. An obscene word expresses emotion. When we use the word 'pig,' we are not meaning that literally. We are trying to express emotion. . . . We are on trial because we are trying to wake America up. We are on trial because we are trying to wake it up emotionally, because it turned us all into machines. . . . So the people at this table are trying to wake it up, and the only way we can wake it up is by screaming, yelling, standing on our heads, doing whatever we can do. That's what we tried to do during the trial. That's what our defense was." (*Seed* [Chicago underground paper], Vol. 4, No. 13).

above, reason and knowledge, it is to treat humans as less than human. People are neither mechanical brains nor unthinking animals. Only humans with the attributes of both thought and feeling can tear down the rotting old society and construct a truly human new one. And the language that is used must always symbolize this vision of humankind.

5. "Making" the Revolution

THE ONE-SIDED stress upon man as subject as against man as part of mankind and of nature, leads directly to the notion that human will alone can decide all, regardless of objective conditions. This is what is known as voluntarism, the belief that one need merely have the will to do things, to "make" the revolution, and pronto, it can be made. The logic of this position taken to its absurd extreme would be to accuse Marx and Engels of not being real revolutionists because they did not make the revolution in their own day.

Man makes his own history, that is true. But as Karl Marx pointed out, he does not make it out of the whole cloth, only from that which is available to him at any given time. Men cannot accomplish what is impossible. Try as they did, the utopians in previous centuries could not establish new social orders based on brotherhood. The time was not yet ripe for that. They could dream of such a society, and dreams are of tremendous importance and play a great role in mankind's progress, but they could not yet realize it. The time can be "seized", but only for that which the objective material forces of society has made possible.

There are a number of important objective reasons for the inclination of many young radicals to place their sole stress on the subjective factor and to adopt a voluntarist approach to the struggle. In the first place, conditions are not what they were in the days of the early utopians or of Marx and Engels. From the viewpoint of the material productive forces of society the United States is riper for social revolution and for a communist society than any country in the world. What is lacking is man's state of mind, his consciousness of the need for revolutionary change. In other words, what is lacking is a conscious *subjective* force strong enough to alter objective reality.* But this lack of a mass anti-capitalist and socialist consciousness is a part of the objective picture and cannot be altered by mere wishful thinking alone, or by a small minority trying to force its will on the majority, or to replace the majority. It is the big, big problem that revolutionists confront in this country. It cannot be solved by succumbing to feelings of frustration or despair, but by ever greater conscious efforts to change the thinking of people by helping them draw the necessary conclusions from the experiences of the struggle itself.

The over-ripe material conditions for revolutionary change in the United States in contrast to the as yet underdeveloped state of mass consciousness of its need, is the underlying cause for the many bizarre features of the youth rebellion and the generational gap. The youthful impatience is understandable; the desire to "make the revolution," praiseworthy; fears of what may happen if the crisis of the system is not resolved in a revolutionary way, real; yet none of these offer answers to the problem we face.

Voluntarism is also a reaction to the tendency of some to use the lack of mass revolutionary consciousness as an excuse for sitting on their hands passively waiting for things to change. Che Guevara had contemptuously referred to this as "waiting until in some mechanical way all necessary objective and subjective conditions are given [for revolution] without working to accelerate them." This tendency is expressed in an exclusive concentration on partial demands, particularly economic ones, and a deliberate avoidance of more complex controversial political issues around which the beginnings of political class conscious-

---

*"You, for example, have created an enormous material base in the United States, an enormous capacity for production, an extraordinarily developed technology. But nonetheless in the midst of this society, much selfishness has been created, there are many misunderstandings, many privileges. You have acquired, you have developed the complete material base to live under communism, but since you have developed it under the laws of capitalism, you have at the same time developed the individualism and selfishness which makes a very different mentality from that needed to live in a communist society" (Fidel Castro, "Interview").

ness alone can be created. Even militant trade unionists suffer from this "practical" approach which, because it never leaves the realm of reformist practice, can never create anything but reformist consciousness. It only strengthens the illusion that the system can be *made* to change itself. Thus, struggle alone cannot create socialist consciousness; the struggle must be imbued with socialist ideals. Yet without struggle the masses cannot learn from their own experiences, for "the masses learn from life and not from books" (Lenin, "Differences in the European Labor Movement", p. 348).

Another factor that feeds subjective voluntarist moods is the dogmatic denial that new times and new conditions require new approaches to strategy and tactics. Methods of struggle highly suitable in one period may become highly unsuitable in another, and vice versa. Jean Paul Sartre has noted that the actions of French students in the May-June 1968 upheaval were greatly influenced by the Vietnamese people's struggle. "It had previously seemed impossible that the Vietnamese could resist successfully such an enormous military machine and win. Yet that is what they did and by doing so they completely changed the horizon of French students, among others. They now knew that there were possibilities that remained unknown. Not that everything was possible, but that one can only know something is impossible once one has tried it and failed" ("Interview").

Sartre is accurate in his description of the mood of young radicals. The Cuban Revolution, too, left the same kind of imprint. While it is necessary to reject crude attempts artificially to imitate success achieved under quite different circumstances—and we have had our share of that over the years!—it is still necessary to recognize that vast social changes have made new tactical approaches and forms of struggle both possible and necessary.

The crisis of the world capitalist system has brought into being an atmosphere highly charged with tensions and social crises. Under certain conditions nearly any one of them could be the spark to ignite the flame. Lenin pointed to the Dreyfus Case in France as an example of a minor scadal that produced a major political crisis. But these crises by themselves cannot produce successful revolutions. They require the intervention of the subjective conscious element in the form of a revolutionary Marxist vanguard capable of imbuing the spontaneous movement with socialist consciousness and the will to revolution and of applying a strategy and tactics capable of uniting the widest masses. Where such a revolutionary subjective force exists it becomes possible to weld alliances formerly believed impossible. In the United States, for example, the revolt of the students and intellectuals indicates that in the very social strata that the ruling class formerly considered safe, in fact, among those it considered its idealogues, its keepers of the faith, the icons are now being smashed.

There is still another reason for the rise in subjective moods as expressed in existentialism and voluntarism. World War II and the Nuremburg trials that followed made the world more conscious of the tremendous responsibilities that individuals must assume for their social actions. The Nazi wholesale slaughter of six million Jewish people and of millions of other East Europeans was condoned and excused by some of the most sadistic mass murderers as being forced on them by orders from above. Others pleaded lack of knowledge. But those who ran the concentration camps and stoked the human ovens knew only too well what they were doing.

So, too, do the Americans in Vietnam today. They know that the genocidal crime of Mylai and many others like it was neither accidental nor incidental. It is the meaning of the American presence in Indochina. Likewise the people in Germany who claimed they knew nothing about the mass slaughters, or the Americans today who try to absolve themselves of responsibility for what is being done to Vietnamese or to black, brown or red peoples of the United States, cannot rid themselves of their responsibilities to mankind and to history for their indifference and silence. They too know the facts, whether they dare admit these to themselves or not. Nor can anyone escape responsibility by claiming "there is nothing I can do." There is always something one can do. There is the moral obligation to say, "No!," to resist by whatever means are possible, to fight back, to revolt, even at the price of great sacrifices, even life itself.

Young radicals tend to feel this moral obligation keenly. When a brutal and debased society tries to brutalize and debase its people, each person has a moral duty to stand up and be counted. It is in this sense that one can and should speak of responsibility to one's conscience. This is not a question of individualism, but of individual responsibility to one's generation and to future generations.

Sometimes a problem of conscience arises even among those already committed to the struggle. History shows that good intentions alone are no safeguard against mistakes. Things go wrong, there are bureaucratic deformations and leaders and organizations lose their way. This occurred during the Stalin period in the Soviet Union, at which time grave crimes and injustices were committed. It has occurred to a lesser extent in other socialist countries as well. It is impossible therefore to shut one's eyes to wrong policies or practices without endangering the very cause in which one believes and for which one fights. Often this is difficult to do. The enemy seeks to use every disagreement within socialist ranks, now that it is a world force, to undermine mass confidence in the cause as such. But the failure to make criticisms for fear of what the enemy may say is to permit mistakes to continue until they are transformed into monstrosities that produce acute internal crises and severe setbacks. It is the theory of spontaneity applied to developments within the movement. It is the belief that spontaneously, on the basis of pure faith alone, mistakes will be corrected, bureaucracy eradicated, injustices undone and things set right.

Had Lenin taken such a view he would never have formed the Bolshevik Party, never broken from the social-democratic betrayers of the Second International, and never had the courage to fight against the majority of the Central Committee of his own party when he thought it wrong. But Lenin was no individualist who set his own views above all others, or acted from personal pique. Many times he accepted decisions he did not agree with, because he believed in discipline and knew that he too could be wrong. But when principle was involved, when the fate of the movement and struggle was at issue, he did not fear standing alone if necessary. To repeat, this has nothing to do with individualism, but involves a sense of *individual responsibility*. Polonius' words in *Hamlet* could be paraphrased to read:

> *This above all*
> *To mankind's cause be true*
> *And it must follow as the night the day*
> *Thou canst not then be false to thyself or any man.*

CHAPTER V

THE STATE AS ENEMY

1. Proudhon's Obsession

TWO RECENT developments have given a new lease on life to the anarchist doctrine of the State. The first of these is the gargantuan increase in State power, which affects more and more every aspect of social life. This concentration of power—political, economic and military—is particularly striking in the United States and is in sharp contrast to the nation's earlier history and tradition.*

The second development is the disillusionment of many with what they consider to be similar tendencies in the socialist countries—overcentralized power, bureaucratic methods, lack of personal liberty, and friction between socialist states. This has led anarchists to charge that socialist states are no better than capitalist ones, and some have even compared the socialist states with fascist ones.

As a consequence, writes Karl Shapiro, "The governments are losing their young. . . . At present we are going through the stage of withdrawal from the old political psychologies of organized governments". Daniel Guérin, in his book *Anarchism*, writes that in the face of recent happenings in socialist countries, "the anarchist critique seems less tendentious, less unjust; sometimes it even seems to have a prophetic ring" (p. 20).

Has history really vindicated the anarchist position of anti-statism?†

---

*"The present tendency of the United States toward greater organization and centralization is a peril to every democratic freedom we know. We are drifting toward a totally organized State that is eventually cemented by a secret police, a standing army, an industrial-scientific autocracy, and a propaganda and communications machine that lies at the very heart of government" (Shapiro).
†"Another term for anarchism is antistatism" (Jacker, p. 1).

First let us remove one aspect of the question from dispute: the State is—always has been and always will be as long as it continues to exist—a social instrument of repression. On this basic proposition Marxism and anarchism are in accord. Their differences are nonetheless fundamental.

The anarchist position on the State is best summed up by its own spokesmen. "The anarchist," writes Guérin, "regards the State as the most deadly of the preconceptions which have blinded men through the ages" (p. 14). He approvingly quotes Max Stirner who, more than a century ago, denounced those who "throughout eternity" are "obsessed by the State." "Every State is a tyranny," said Stirner, "be it the tyranny of a single man or a group. . . . The State has always one purpose: to limit, control, subordinate the individual and subject him to the general purpose" (Guérin, p. 14-15).

Pierre J. Proudhon, the ideological godfather of anarchism, made the most impassioned and detailed of all indictments of government:

> To be governed is to be watched over, inspected, spied on, directed, legislated, closed in, indoctrinated, preached at, controlled, assessed, evaluated, censored, commanded; all by creatures that have neither the right, nor wisdom, nor virtue. . . . To be governed means that at every move, operation, or transaction one is noted, registered, entered in a census, taxed, stamped, priced, assessed, patented, licensed, authorized, recommended, admonished, prevented, reformed, set right, corrected. Government means to be subjected to tribute, trained, ransomed, exploited, monopolized, extorted, pressured, mystified, robbed; all in the name of public utility and the general good. Then, at the first sign of resistance or word of complaint, one is repressed, fined, deported, sacrificed, sold, betrayed, and to cap it all, ridiculed, mocked, outraged, and dishonored. *That* is government, *that* is its justice and its morality! . . . O human personality! How can it be that you have cowered in such subjection for sixty centuries? (Guérin, p. 15-16.)

These statements are sharp and clear. They leave no room for ambiguity: The State is a monstrous abomination; the very embodiment of evil. Its emergence some 6,000 years ago is seen as the original sin, the "obsession" and "preconception" for which mankind has been paying, and from which it has been unable to free itself. "O human personality! How can it be that you have cowered in such subjection for sixty centuries?"

2. As Class Instrument

NEITHER PROUDHON nor his disciples see the State as a social institution within a concrete historic setting, but as an abstraction and aberration. It is something that need not have been had men only been wise enough or morally strong enough to resist the "obsession" and "preconception" that led to their own enslavement. And the sole purpose of the State, as they see it, is the repression of the individual, the human personality.

But not all individuals are victims of State power. In ancient Rome there was no repression for the members of the slave-owning leisure class and its intellectual hangers-on. There was brutal repression for the slaves. In medieval society there was no repression for the aristocracy and for the feudal lords and barons; there was for the serfs. In capitalist society there is no repression for the rich and the ultra-rich; there is for the oppressed, the exploited, the working people, and for all, regardless of class origin, who protest against injustice and join the fight against the system.

The State did not come into being because of "preconceptions", or because evil individuals sought to impose their rule upon other individuals. Nor did it arise from a conflict between abstract man, the individual, and an abstract social environment. It arose for entirely different reasons.

When the growth of the productive forces enabled men to produce a surplus over their barest subsistence needs, it became possible for some to live at the expense of the toil of others. It was then that the State became a necessity.

The State is the natural product of the division of society into conflicting economic classes. Prior to that time there was no need for a repressive social force. In primitive communal society there were chosen chieftains and established rules and norms of conduct, but these were not foisted upon society by a ruling class in its own property interests. There was no ruling class because there were no private property interests.

A military force of some kind was needed by the tribal community to defend it from wild beasts or hostile tribes. This was composed of all able-bodied men. But with the emergence of the class struggle a new type of armed force became necessary. Men were hired as mercenaries and separated from the people. This army was trained to embark on foreign conquest or to intervene against its own people when called upon by the master ruling class. Laws too became necessary to legitimize and institutionalize the given system of property relations as the very *sine qua non* of civilization itself. And courts were established to enforce these laws and a clergy paid to sanctify them.

It can be seen, therefore, that the State arose, not from whim, or obsession, but for well defined historic reasons. James Madison, the "father" of the U.S. Constitution, understood well the role of government as a *class* instrument. "Those who hold and those who are without property," he wrote in the famous No. 10 of his *Federalist Papers*, "have ever formed distinct interests in society." He recognized that "the principal task" of government is "the regulation of these various and interfering interests."

While Madison recognized the need to regulate disputes between different class interests, he was particularly concerned with "the danger that certain groups, particularly the propertyless masses, may fuse into an overbearing majority and sacrifice to its will the the interests of the minority" (Beard, p. 334).

Hence, while governments ostensibly were established to mediate the struggle between the classes in the interests of "society as a whole" in reality, they were established to keep the exploited classes in submission. "Civil government," noted Adam Smith, writing in 1776, "is in reality instituted for the defense of the rich against the poor or of those who have some property against those who have none at all" (Smith, p. 207).*

Nor could it have been otherwise.

---

*"The masters of the Government of the United States are the combined capitalists and manufacturers of the United States" (W. Wilson, pp. 57-58).

Proudhon asked how it was possible that the human personality cowered in subjection for sixty centuries. The answer—and history is replete with examples—is that men and women did not cower in subjection. They fought tyranny and oppression. Nor have their struggles been without consequence. Sure, the State as a repressive social force is still with us. But this is not because history has stood still for sixty centuries.

Men struggling in different historic periods and at different stages of social development could only hope to achieve that which material objective reality made possible. They could not put an end to all forms of State power so long as it was impossible to put an end to all forms of class division and class strife.

So long as the material productive forces of society were still insufficiently developed to meet the full needs of all people, it was utopian to believe that economic classes and the struggle between them could be abolished merely because some dreamed of doing so.

The blows that were struck for freedom could not be aimed at tyranny, oppression, class rule and State power as *abstractions.* They had to be concentrated on the *specific* class enemy of the day—the specific exploiting class in power and its specific form of State rule. And this was so even when the slogans were general ones, aiming to appeal to all the discontented, and when rebelling masses had the illusion that by tearing down the prevailing despotism they would tear down all despotism.

Anarchism fails to understand this historic process. Even when it gives lip service to it, it does so without really grasping its *objective* nature. It tends to view society and history subjectively, as if first came the "preconception," the "obsession," and then the domination of the State. But the historic process is an opposite one. First came the changes in the way men earned their living, in the development of their tools and their productivity. With each qualitative growth in the productive forces of society there came into being, in time, a corresponding qualitative change in social relations (class relations). Different systems of production and exchange and different types of State power arose.

Anarchism makes its appeal to eternal truth, but truth is rooted in reality, in the material conditions of life. Truth is concrete. As terrible as was classical slave society for the slaves, it still marked a great leap forward for mankind. For the first time man had "tamed" nature sufficiently to be able to maintain a leisure class. And with everything negative that has flowed from the division of society into classes, it would be one-sided and wrong to fail to see the historic progression involved.

Today, for the first time in human history, a classless, State-less society is within man's grasp. For the first time it has become possible to complete the cycle of class societies which began when primitive communal society ended.

Tribal society was collective in character, with neither ruling class nor repressive social agency. This was not because men willed it to be such. *It had to be.* Man's primitive relation to nature, the general conditions of scarcity, made cooperation and collective-cooperative life a matter of life or death.

Once again a collectivist, cooperative society is becoming a matter of life or death for humankind. The breathtaking advances in science and technology, the ability to produce abundance for all in highly developed countries, no longer give historic justifica-tion for the continued division of society into conflicting classes. Production today is highly social in character. No man can live any longer on what he alone produces. The latest revolution in science and technology, the role of automation and computeriza-tion, make the private (corporate) ownership of the productive plant and its continued use for private profit an anachronism which becomes more anti-social with each passing year, en-dangering the continued existence of life on earth.

A higher form of society, a communist society, based on abundance and the complete elimination of classes and the State, is now at last within mankind's reach. To have foreseen and understood this historic process was the great contribution that Marxism made to social science.

Engels, in 1883, wrote a Preface to a new German edition of the *Communist Manifesto.* He summed up its essence in one para-graph:

"The basic thought running through the *Manifesto*—that economic production and the structure of society of every historical epoch necessarily arising therefrom constitute the foundation for the political and intellectual history of that epoch; that consequently (ever since the dissolution of the primeval communal ownership of land) all history has been a history of class struggles, of struggles between exploited and exploiting, between dominated and dominating classes at various stages of social development; that this struggle, however, has now reached a stage where the exploited and oppressed class (the proletariat) can no longer emancipate itself from the class which exploits and oppresses it (the bourgeiosie), without at the same time forever freeing the whole of society from exploitation, oppression and class struggles" ("Preface to the Communist Manifesto," 1883, pp. 132-33).

3. An A-historical View of History

THE ACHILLES heel of anarchist thinking is its a-historical approach. More concretely, it is its failure to recognize that as long as society is divided into classes it is the class struggle that is the main motive force of social change. To try to abolish the State without first ending class strife in society, is to try to abolish an effect without first abolishing its cause.

This obsession with the State—every and all States—as the root *cause* of all social oppression, leads anarchism away from the solid ground of class analysis into the murky swamp of petty-bourgeois subjectivism and individualism.

One need but read anarchist literature to recognize how little thought is actually given to what it really takes to do away with State power. Karl Shapiro, whom we quoted previously, says that the young were "going through a stage of withdrawal from the old political psychologies of organized government."

What does this really mean? Does Shapiro truly believe that the formation of counter-culture collectives, or the stress on "do your own thing," or on civil disobedience, will weaken, let alone destroy, the growing concentration of political, economic and military power in the hands of the corporate giants that run the government? If so, he is a naive man indeed.

Shapiro believes that Gandhi showed us the way. "One nonviolent man, like Gandhi or Christ," he writes, "can change history." But how did Christ change history? Shapiro does not tell us. Has there been more Christian love, less oppression and less human carnage? As for Gandhi, Shapiro lauds his abhorrence of violence and his love for his enemies. He gives an example of Gandhi's moral influence upon others by telling us of Vinobe Bhave, "the greatest living disciple of Gandhi." Bhave, according to Shapiro, "travels throughout India asking land for the peasantry from the great landlords and receiving it, says: 'I desire to humiliate neither the rich nor the poor.'" From this Shapiro draws a moral: "This is the opposite of communist expropriation or of capitalist competition. Without a complete bond of love between the giver and the recipient there can be no permanent guarantee of peace between the possessor and the dispossessed."

Shapiro does not tell us how much land the starving, poverty-stricken landless Indian peasantry has received by this humiliating hat-in-hand begging from the "great landlords." He must forgive us if we remain skeptical.

Nor do we share his enthusiasm for a permanent peace between the "possessors and the dispossessed." We are against such a peace. There can be no peace as long as society is divided into possessors and dispossessed. To preach social peace between the rich and the poor is to advise passive acceptance of a system built on exploitation and oppression.

Yes, begging for parcels of land from the high and mighty certainly is the "opposite of communist expropriation," although we disagree that it is the opposite of "capitalist competition." There is nothing anti-capitalist about it.

Most anarchists would probably disagree with Shapiro's embrace of the "love thy enemy" doctrine in the name of anarchism. Yet all anarchists share his basic defect, which is to think in individualist and not in class terms. They see oppression and exploitation *only* as moral questions, not as questions of class society and class relations. And because of this they think they can successfully conduct the struggle along individualist lines as against class lines.

But the war against entrenched power and wealth is a long,

difficult, arduous struggle, requiring perseverance, discipline, and the readiness of the individual to subordinate himself and his ego to the will of the larger revolutionary collective.

To fail to understand this is to find oneself, as anarchists all too frequently do, on the wrong side of the battle front. And this tends to occur at critical points in the struggle: when the going is toughest, the need for sacrifice the greatest, and the stakes the highest.

Anarchists reject all State power as a matter of moral principle. But from a class point of view this is untenable. What is lost sight of is the very fact that the class war is a political war and that the concrete prize fought over is the State. To give up this prize in advance is tantamount to giving up the struggle against both the System and its State.

Only by possessing State power can the bourgeoisie impose its will and defend its economic system against all antagonists. And only by creating a revolutionary counterforce capable of winning and holding State power is it possible to destroy capitalism root and branch and to restructure society along revolutionary collectivist lines, with the aim of abolishing *all* classes—the proletariat as well—and with them the need for all repressive State authority.

4. "Third World" and the Anarchist Dilemma

THERE ARE many examples of how untenable the anarchists' abstract opposition to all State power is, and how reactionary it can be in practice.

Let us start with the situation in the so-called "Third World." Here, peoples oppressed by imperialism for generations have been rising in wrath, demanding the right to govern themselves free of all foreign interference. Since World War II, a majority of oppressed colonial peoples have won the formal right to political independence, but not yet their right to *full* self-development.

U. S. imperialism has sought to undermine the independence of the new States and to make them subservient to its interests. More than a century of domination of Latin America has taught it that *formal* political independence need not be an insuperable barrier to actual imperialist subjugation.

While imperialism is much weaker than it formerly was, challenged as it is by an ever stronger socialist world and scores of nations fighting for liberation, it nonetheless still has financial, economic and military resources with which to try to subvert the new States and to turn them into its pliable instruments. These intrigues have not been without success. A string of the newly born States has been the victim of counter-revolutionary coups and has been incorporated, temporarily at least, into the Wall Street empire.

Only where strong disciplined revolutionary power was established, resting on the armed might of the working people, have the anti-imperialist revolutions succeeded in consolidating their independence. And this has been so particularly where the national democratic revolution was followed by a socialist revolution.

The fate of revolutionary socialist Cuba would have been that of Guatemala, Guyana and the Dominican Republic were it not for the social revolution that nationalized not only imperialist holdings but also those of the national bourgeoisie; established close links with the Soviet Union and the other socialist lands, and prepared itself militarily and otherwise to face whatever came its way from the Colossus of the North only 90 miles away.

Vietnam is the supreme example of how a valiant people is ready to fight for national independence and statehood, despite genocidal death and destruction rained upon it. Let someone try to tell the Vietnamese that their war for national liberation, for the right to choose their own form of government and social system, is not worth the sacrifice! Let someone try to tell them that there is no difference between the puppet regime in Saigon and the people's socialist government in Hanoi! Not even an anarchist would dare utter such nonsense.

Whenever anarchists leave abstractions and face reality they confront a dilemma. If they stick to the abstract principles of anti-statism they find themselves on the wrong side of the battlefront. But to get on the revolutionary side of the front they must compromise their abstract principles. This is their quandary.

The anarchist predicament is discussed by Horowitz. He points out that the Gandhi pacifist variant of anarchism was the instrumentality through which national independence for India was achieved. "But in that very act," he notes, "emerged the Indian *State.* And to ensure the success of the revolutionary movement meant the consecration and sanctioning of the coercive State after the revolution. The use of armies, policemen, and 'agents of the State,' had to be given a large priority" (p. 55).

This is certainly true. If there is any criticism on this score it is that the Indian revolution did not go far enough, was not revolutionary enough. It did not give land to the peasants and arms to the people. It did not take over the large imperialist holdings and did not establish a democratic dictatorship of workers and peasants that would guarantee the fullest development of India free of all imperialist interference. In the world of today, anti-imperialist, national democratic revolutions must go *all the way* if the imperialists asked to leave by the front door are not to return by the back door. They must be driven out so that they never return.

Horowitz ends his discussion of the anarchist quandary by wryly commenting: "It is perhaps in the nature of anarchism that it can never have any real 'victory' without sacrificing its principles" (p. 55).

5. The Lesson of the Paris Commune

THE GERMS of this anarchist dilemma have made themselves evident in every crisis involving the question of State power. The very first of these was that of the Paris Commune of 1871. Having overpowered federal troops and taken possession of the city in the name of the working class, the Parisians established their own government. The Paris Commune did away with the standing army, substituting in its place a people's militia. It made all elected officials subject to recall, established free and general education, separated church from State, reorganized the police, and set top limits on salaries for elected government personnel.

This was a different type of government, but it was a government nonetheless. (Marx spoke of it as the prototype of the working-class governments to come.) Its very formation, therefore, created certain problems of conscience for the followers of Proudhon and Bakunin who were active in the Commune. While compelled to compromise their anti-statist views and to accept the Commune with its elected officials, laws, regulations, etc., anarchist influences did have a baneful effect upon the basic class outlook of the Commune, bending this in an unrealistic petty-bourgeois direction.

The single gravest error of the Commune, the error which was to cost its life and the lives of tens of thousands of brave Communards only three months later, was the failure to march immediately upon Versailles, the seat of the national government. Had it done so, the reactionary bourgeoisie would not have had the time to reorganize its forces for the counter-revolutionary assault upon Paris.

Thiers, the head of the Versailles government, and members of his cabinet, were in Paris on March 18, the day of insurrection. They could have been arrested by the revolutionary government without difficulty. Later, Thiers admitted that had the Commune attacked Versailles promptly, his government could not have withstood it (Foster, 1955, p. 93). The Communards did not march on Versailles, or arrest Thiers, because they feared civil war—as if the civil war had not already begun!

This was the costliest error of the Commune, but not the only one of like nature. It did not confiscate the three billion francs held by the Bank of France; was too soft on Versailles agents, spies and traitors operating with impunity within the city; did not act firmly against the old officer corps, etc.

All these errors flowed from one basic source—an underestimation of the nature of the class struggle, a failure to recognize that the bourgeoisie would stop at nothing to regain power. The old ruling class must be crushed or the revolution will be crushed. It is one or the other. Never truer were the words of Goethe:

"Thou must win or lose, suffer or triumph, either anvil or hammer be."*

6. The Spanish Revolution of 1873

ONE MAY forgive the Communards for their soft-heartedness and illusions. They, after all, were the first to "storm the heavens." But if the world revolutionary movement has learned something from the mistakes of the Commune, the anarchists have not. They find themselves in a new crisis of conscience with every new revolutionary crisis of power.

Two years after the Paris Commune, the Spanish anarchists were caught in a like predicament. The bourgeois revolution of 1873 had swept the Monarchy out of power and substituted for it a federal republican form of government. The anarchists were at a loss as to what to do. They arrived at a "highly characteristic" decision. They "refused to give any general support to the Federalist movement, but they raised no objections to their local groups or individual members cooperating with it." They even permitted their local organizations to participate in the cantonal provincial governments.

In this way they tried to eat their cake and have it too. They thought they could take advantage of the situation for themselves "without compromising either their principles or their freedom of action" (Brenan, p. 376).

Thus, in this crisis too, the anarchists could not disentangle themselves from the web of their own anti-statist contradictions. Life was demanding a clear stand as between absolute monarchy

---

*"A revolution is certainly the most authoritarian thing there is; it is the act whereby one part of the population imposes its will upon the other part by means of rifles, bayonets, and cannon—authoritarian means, if such there be at all; and if the victorious party does not want to have fought in vain, it must maintain its rule by means of the terror which its arms inspire in the reactionaries. Would the Paris Commune have lasted a single day if it had not made use of this authority of the armed people against the bourgeoisie? *Should we not, on the contrary, reproach it for not having used it freely enough?"* (emphasis added; Engels, "On Authority," p. 485).

and a federal republic. The anarchists could not completely dodge this issue. So they temporized, hedged and decided to let everyone do his own thing. It soon was too late for meaningful action. Carlist monarchist reaction swept Spain.

7. Anarchists and the Spanish Civil War

THE SPANISH Civil War (1936-39) again found the anarchists in an ambivalent position. They had opposed the Popular Front on traditional grounds, although most of their own followers had helped vote it into power. Even when Franco's fascist legions, with the direct military aid of fascist Germany and Italy, began their insurrection against the democratic republic, the anarchists did not alter their position. They were against the fascists, but they were also against the government Franco was determined to overthrow, and against anti-fascist unity to defeat the fascist armies.

When the other anti-fascist forces appealed for unity and discipline, in the formation of a common front of struggle and a single anti-fascist army, the anarchists countered with posters urging "the organization of indiscipline." They distributed a piece of literature among the anarchist militia in Aragón, which read in part: "We do not accept the militarization because it would lead to an obvious danger. We do not recognize military formations because that is the negation of Anarchism. Winning the war does not mean winning the revolution. Technology and strategy are important in the present war, not discipline which presupposes a negation of the personality" (Ibarruri, p. 285). How it was possible to have either technology or strategy without discipline, the anarchists did not trouble to explain.

Many anarchists fought bravely and well, but many rejected all discipline as a matter of principle. If there was a temporary lull in fighting on some front, it was not unusual to see anarchist militiamen pick up their belongings and hit the road—for home, some other front, or wherever their interest or curiosity led them. The anarchists opposed building fortifications, whether at the battle fronts or in defense of the cities, and here and there anarchist troops were even reported to be fraternizing with fascist troops. In one area on the Aragón front, according to Herbert Matthews who covered the republican side of the war for the *New York Times,* "football games had actually been arranged between the lines of troops of both sides—and this while the militia of the central front and the Biscayan litoral were being bled white under the pounding guns of the Italian and Moorish legions" (Landis, p. 256).

Later, events compelled sections of the anarchist movement to veer away from earlier judgments, to enter the united front against Franco, and even to accept posts of responsibility in the Popular Front Government. How extensive were these changes can be seen by the new constitution adopted by the most influential of the anarchist organizations, the Iberian Anarchist Federation known as FAI, approximately one year after the civil war began. It declared in its preamble:

> The Revolution must be oriented and directed. The FAI must give its movement a new structure accepting the practices that are necessary to achieve victory and that are demanded by the special conditions in which the war and revolution place us. Subordinated individually and collectively to our supreme aim we must be coherent, disciplined and daring in action. . . . The FAI must have a uniform political line that embraces all aspects of social and political life, so that it may anticipate "how" it will act at any moment and in any circumstances (*Volunteer for Liberty,* August 1937, Vol.1, No. 11).

Commenting on the new constitution's call for stern discipline and a single party line, the publication of the International Brigade reminded its readers: "Those who recall the Anarchist posters calling for the organization of indiscipline, will have some hint of the internal revolution this decision symbolizes" (*ibid.*).

An equally striking illustration of the "internal revolution" is to be seen in the changed attitude toward the State. As late as two months after the civil war began, the anarchists were still of the opinion that the government was unimportant, that it could be ignored, and that the only thing that really counted was taking over the economy. On September 3, 1936, an article appeared in the *Information Bulletin* of FAI and the CNT (the large anarcho-syndicalist trade union federation) entitled, "The Futility of Government." This suggested that the economic expropriation which was taking place would lead *ipso facto* to "the liquidation of the bourgeois State, which would die of asphyxiation" (Guérin, p. 128).

"This underestimation of government," writes Guérin, . was very rapidly reversed and the Spanish anarchists suddenly became governmentalists . . . . The anarchists ended up by accepting portfolios in two governments: first in Catalonia and subsequently in Madrid."

They became "governmentalists" with a vengeance. Even before they accepted portfolios in the government, their *real* position toward government was indicated in the FAI-POUM (the Trotzkyist Party) attempt to overthrow the Popular Front Government of Catalonia. On May 3, 1937, in the middle of an enemy offensive in the North, the anarcho-Trotzkyists began their armed rebellion. They submitted an ultimatum to the government which demanded the following governmental posts: "The Ministry of War; the Ministries of Industry, Transportation, Trade, Finances, Agriculture; the posts of Chief of Police, Police Commissar of Barcelona and all other important posts" (Ibarruri, p. 281).

In effect, this attempt at "revolution," was in reality an attempt at counter-revolution. So it was understood by Franco and the fascists whose agents claimed credit for the "disorders." On May 11, 1937, Faupel, the German Ambassador who maintained close contact with Franco, wrote a report to Hitler about the May rebellion in Barcelona. "Concerning the disorders in Barcelona," he informed *Der Feuhrer*, "Franco has told me that the street fighting was provoked by his agents." One of Franco's agents in Barcelona "had reported that the tension between Anarchists and Communists in Barcelona was so great that it could well end in street fighting."

The Generalissimo told me [continued the German Ambassador's report] that at first he doubted the agent's reports, but later they were confirmed by other agents. Originally he did not intend to take advantage of this possibility until military operations had been established in Catalonia. But since the Reds had recently attacked Teruel to aid the

Government of Euzcadi, he thought the time was right for the outbreak of disorders in Barcelona" (Ibarruri, p. 282).

Thus, the anarchist switch to participation in the Popular Front Government did not come without travail. And when it did it only accentuated the crisis within anarchist ranks, both in Spain and abroad. The International Workers' Association, the anarchist international federation, of which the CNT was the largest and most important affiliate, held a special congress in Paris in June 1937, "at which the anarcho-syndicalist trade union center was reproached for participating in government and for the concessions it had made in consequence." Guerin reports, "The CNT was enraged and brought about the resignation of the secretary of the International Workers' Association, Pierre Besnard" (Guérin, pp. 128-29).

Guérin is highly critical of the Spanish anarchist's "change of heart." He explains the reasons that motivated it.

As the fascist powers increased their support for Franco, the anti-fascist struggle degenerated into a real war, a total war of the classical type. The libertarians could only take part in it by abandoning more and more of their principles, both political and military. They reasoned, falsely, that the victory of the Revolution could only be assured by first winning the war and, as Santillan* was to admit, they "sacrificed everything" to the war (Guérin, p. 129).

What does Guérin mean when he says, "the anti-fascist struggle *degenerated* into a *real* war." Of course it was a real war. The planes, tanks, cannons, bombs, bullets were real indeed. So were the Moorish and Italian fascist legions and German Nazi participation and aid.

The use of the word "degenerated," as well as the pejorative use of the phrase "total war of the classical type," is meant apparently to deny the democratic and revolutionary character of the war. It is as if one were to accuse the National Liberation Front of South Vietnam of abandoning its revolutionary princi-

---

*Diego Abad de Santillan, FAI leader, who in his book *Por que Perdimos la Guerra* (Why We Lost the War, Buenos Aires, 1940), admitted "his tie with Jose Antonio Primo de Rivera, the founder of the Falange" (Ibarruri, p. 282).

ples because it places priority upon and sacrifices all for the winning of the war. Winning the war is the most revolutionary thing the Vietnamese people can do, as its own people and the imperialists so well understand.

The Spanish Civil War of 1936-39 had the same significance for its time as does the Vietnam War—now Indochina War—for our time. The victory of the fascist legions in Spain led inevitably to World War II, for it encouraged the fascist states to believe they could continue their aggressions with impunity. A victory for U.S. imperialism in Indochina today would have similar world consequences. It would encourage U.S. armed intervention against other peoples fighting for their freedom and against other socialist states or socialist revolutions.

In concluding his section on the Spanish Civil War, Guérin admits: "The defeat of the Spanish Revolution deprived anarchism of its only foothold in the world. It came out of this trial crushed, dispersed, to some extent, discredited" (Guérin, p. 144).

This is certainly true, but for reasons other than those seen by Guérin. He believes anarchism was discredited because some departed from its abstract rhetorical concepts. It was discredited because once again, at an historic moment of truth, it had been found wanting. And even when it tried to correct its course, it was too heavily laden with its own ideological encumbrances to be able to make a meaningful turn. Thus, Barcelona, the traditional stronghold of Spanish anarchism, fell to fascist arms without any serious attempt at armed resistance; while Madrid, where Communist influence was strongest, held out against the hunger and bombs of a cruel military siege that lasted for 26 long months, from November 1936 to January 1939.

Despite the clear-minded principled program and heroic example of the Spanish Communists in the life and death struggle to halt fascism, Guérin blames them for the fascist victory. There is something strange in all this. Whenever a setback or defeat takes place there are some who rush to blame the Communists, but when revolutions succeed, as they have in fourteen countries of the world, the Communists are damned by the same people for taking state power. Whatever differences people may have with the Communists, the fact has to be recognized that only where Communists hold state power has the bourgeoisie been expropriated and is a new social system based on collective ownership being built. This is true despite all the imperfections, blunders and distortions that accompany the creation of anything completely new. Referring to Alexander Berkman's and Emma Goldman's carping criticisms of the early Soviet state, Irving Horowitz made a penetrating comment. He wrote, "One is always a bit discontented by the type of criticism that can never be wrong because it is always dealing in the realm of what *ought* to be" (p. 60).

8. The Socialist States

IT IS Guérin's central contention, as it is of most anarchists, that the experience of the socialist countries has vindicated the anarchist criticism of Marxism. Bakunin has been proven right, they believe, and Marx wrong.

Without doubt the building of a new society has proven more complex and difficult than first imagined. We now know that the habits of centuries are not easily shed and constantly reassert themselves in new ways. Bureaucracy, too, is a real menace and not easily overcome. Socialist countries have been plagued with bureaucratic excesses, with cults of personality and of mediocrity, and with remnants of nationalism and chauvinism.

All these faults exist and cannot be condoned. They have led and can still lead to grave reverses for socialism. Nor will they disappear spontaneously. It will require deeper theoretical probing and political struggle for their eradication. But in order to do this it is necessary to see them in historic perspective and in the context of the worldwide struggle of our time. This the anarchists are incapable of doing.

It should not be forgotten that the revolution came first to a single country and one economically underdeveloped. With the birth of the Soviet State the class struggle took on a fierce international character as well. The origin of the Cold War, as has been pointed out by others, goes all the way back to the Russian

Revolution and the attempt to strangle it in its infancy. This international class war, for that is what the Cold War is, has become far more intense and protracted with the rise of the other socialist States. Imperialism, and in the first place U. S. imperialism, has never acquiesced to the existence of a new social system which, by its very nature, is a constant challenge to capitalism in the rest of the world. Capitalism seeks to destroy it. If this cannot be done all at once, it is attempted piecemeal. Socialism must be "contained," new revolutions must be kept from succeeding, the socialist countries divided among themselves, their contradictions and weaknesses taken advantage of, and so forth and so on.

The fact that the revolution came first of all to the countries of lesser economic development, and has yet to come to one of the big, highly developed western countries, has compelled the socialist States to take the path of forced economic development. And we now know that the struggle to overcome underdevelopment is far more difficult, as Fidel Castro has noted, than the struggle for power itself.

These historic peculiarities of the way the process of world revolution has developed should not be used to excuse bureaucratic distortions, but must be taken into account as objective facts. Anarchists see centralized State power as the original sin from which all others stem. But had Proudhon's and Bakunin's anti-statist views prevailed there would be no socialism being built anywhere. In the world of today the only viable alternative to capitalist-imperialist States is socialist States, and not the completely stateless society the anarchists advocate. There can be no escaping the fact that the centralized socialist State—yes, the dictatorship of the proletariat in one form or another—is absolutely imperative so long as the struggle between the old and the new systems has not yet been resolved conclusively on a world scale. The struggle for greater internal democracy and personal liberty in socialist countries must be seen in this context. Seen outside of it, it degenerates into petty-bourgeois liberalism.

It is precisely the *dual* need of the socialist countries for strong State power *and* for the greatest involvement of the people themselves in the building of a society *without privileges for anyone,* that creates the contradiction so difficult to resolve. That is why the anarchist criticism of socialist countries, even when valid in one respect or another, is fundamentally invalid. Its premise is false. It seeks the weakening and destruction of the socialist State vis-à-vis its imperialist foes and not its strengthening. When Guérin points to Algeria and Yugoslavia as examples where more democratic forms of workers' management are emerging, he only adds to our feeling of unease. It is questionable whether Algeria is actually building socialism and we have grave doubts as to where Yugoslavia is heading.

As previously noted, the big divide between Marxism and anarchism is not over the objective of a classless, stateless society. Nor is it over concern for the individual. It is over the question of the class struggle and the need to recognize its imperatives.

Proudhon's passionate diatribe against the horrors of the State previously quoted is typical of the abstract anarchist, a-historical conception of the State. But the State can never be fought as an abstraction, only as the concrete embodiment of the rule of a given class. To fight it as an abstraction is to tilt at windmills.

CHAPTER VI

VIOLENCE, TERRORISM AND GUERRILLA WAR

1. "America, the Violent"

THE NEW YORK *Times Book Review* of Sunday, April 12, 1970, carried reviews of seven new books on violence. Titles ranged from "Our Violent Society," "The History of Violence in America," "America the Violent," "Violence in America," to "On Violence." Lewis A. Coser, the reviewer, notes that violence has replaced poverty as the current issue of concern—at least among publishers.

Coser disagrees with those who claim this country to be *the* most violent in the world. But no one can deny that it is one of the most violent.

England, Japan and West Germany are, next to the United States, the most heavily industrialized countries in the world. Together they have a population of 214 million. Among these 214 million, there are 135 gun murders a year. Among the 200 million people of the United States there are 6,500 gun murders a year—about *forty-eight times* as many. Philadelphia alone has about the same number of criminal homicides as England, Scotland and Wales combined—as many in a city of two million (and a city of brotherly love, at that) as in a nation of 45 million. (Schlesinger, p. 43).

Our police are among the most brutal. An English bobby, for example, carries no gun, but in this country police often shoot first and ask questions after. It is also commonplace for crime suspects—especially when young, Black, Brown or Indian—to be mercilessly beaten and maltreated, with confessions wrung from them by sadistic torture, whether guilty or not.

Our history as a nation is replete with violence. The Indian peoples were subjected to genocidal slaughter and then herded into reservations to starve. The Africans were brought here in chains and have been kept in chains ever since. In the century since their "emancipation" more than five thousand have been recorded as lynched, i.e., wantonly and sadistically murdered by racist mobs. The frontiers of the United States have been ruthlessly and violently expanded with lands stolen wholesale from both Indians and Mexicans. In 1898 the United States grabbed Cuba, the Philippines and Puerto Rico. The latter is still in its clutches and only Cuba is truly free.

The United States is the only country in the world to have used the atom bomb. Assuming the need to drop it at all—which we do not—some sparsely populated region of the earth could have been found to demonstrate the awesome power of the new weapon. Instead, it was deliberately and cold-bloodedly dropped on two of the most densely populated cities in the world. And in Vietnam today this country is guilty of a thousand Mylai massacres, for its policy and practice are genocidal. Nor is it accidental that its most barbaric atrocities are commited against colored peoples.

The history of class war in the United States is also one of bloody encounters. When a striker or demonstrator is shot or killed in a West European country a great hue and cry is raised. In the United States it is taken as one of those things—another fatality, a statistic to be computed.

Two examples out of hundreds should suffice. During the short span of two years (1934-36) in which the great union organizing drive was gathering momentum, 88 workers lost their lives in strike struggles. And in the past two years, a number of young Black Panthers have been shot to death by police in so-called "shoot-outs" in which the shooting was nearly always on only one side.

The issue of violence became a matter of widespread public concern following each of the savage political assassinations of recent years—John F. Kennedy, Malcolm X, Robert Kennedy, Martin Luther King Jr.—and especially following the fiery wave of ghetto rebellions. But the concern has not been all of the same kind.

Faced with mounting discontent and a growing radical mood, our rulers are concerned less with reducing violence by reducing or ending repression, and more with using the issue of violence demagogically to win popular approval for even greater repression. This is the true meaning of the "crime in our streets" issue.

Sure, there is growing crime in the streets. The causes for this lie in poverty, joblessness, racism, and the highly profitable, police-protected narcotics traffic, as many must know. But the issue of crime is cunningly used to obtain the means for escalating violence. The size of the police force is being increased everywhere: millions of dollars are being appropriated to store more tear gas, mace, shot-guns, rifles and every which type of "anti-riot" weaponry; U.S. soldiers, the National Guard and U.S. marshals are being trained for "domestic emergencies"; the armed occupation of the ghettos tightens; and college and high-school premises are invaded with the permanent presence of the police.

A new federal "anti-conspiracy" law is now on the books, aiming to prevent people from crossing state lines to participate in centrally organized demonstrations. This was what the Chicago Conspiracy Trial was all about.

The FBI is asking for and will get additional tens of millions of dollars to combat so-called "subversion." This is to be done by tapping more phones, bugging more homes, following more people, snooping through more wastepaper baskets and garbage cans, and infiltrating more organizations with more government stool pigeons and agent provocateurs. President Nixon's shameless efforts to pack the Supreme Court with the most racist, reactionary judges he can find are part of this same rush to greater reaction and repression.

The pretext for all this is the so-called danger of "Left violence." Ruling class repression and terror are being passed off as protective counter measures, and not as the original and prime cause for whatever measures people do take to defend themselves and their rights.

It is true, unfortunately, that there has been an excessive preoccupation with rhetoric about violence in a few sections of the new radicalism. There has also been an inclination on the part of a small number of young people to play the dangerous game of individual counter-terror. Taking advantage of this, the media have misled a considerable number of people into believing that the violence comes from the Left and not from the ruling class.

To see how unfounded this illusion is one needs but recall that the new radicalism started out as a movement dedicated to nonviolence, even to the extreme of turning this into a form of gospel. Despite hundreds of police and racist mob attacks on the early civil rights and peace movements, these were never met with physical resistance of any sort. Even when demonstrators and activists were illegally arrested they did not resist; they simply went limp, refusing to cooperate with the police.

In the South, violence took the form of organized murder and terror. The roster of young martyrs who paid with their lives is evidence of this. It was a terror perpetrated, directed, or aided and abetted by local authorities with the knowledge and connivance of federal authority. None of the much heralded civil rights laws made any substantial difference.

Violence was the order of the day. This was not the spontaneous violence of suffering Black people against unbearable conditions, nor was it the violence of civil rights activists determined to defend their rights and their lives; it was the calculated organized violence and terror of responsible respectable forces of "law and order."

Finally the dam of patience broke. The new radicals were compelled to reevaluate their basic approach to violence and nonviolence. It was amply clear that knowledge on the part of the police and racist mobs that the Movement would not lift an arm in physical self-defense did not deter them from violence; it only spurred them to greater violence. The question therefore arose: Would not a policy of mass armed self-defense, publicly proclaimed, do more to curb cowardly attacks than that of meekly turning the other cheek?

The questioning went even deeper than that. As wholesale violence was being employed to hold back democratic reforms of a purely liberal kind, what could be expected from the ruling powers when demands of a radical kind were made? Experience had also taught an increasing number of the young militants that racism and oppression are endemic to the very nature of U.S. capitalism and cannot be ended without ending the system itself. But this posed an even tougher question: If threatened, would not the system defend its class interests and prerogatives by *every* means at its disposal?

Thus the doctrine of nonviolence became challenged on even broader grounds.

Two additional factors led to this. The first of these was the war in Vietnam. This war was so patently an unprovoked imperialist assault upon the sovereignty of a small people that opposition to it on the part of the new radicals was instantaneous. It soon was recognized that while the war was *unjust* on the part of the United States, it was *just* on the part of the Vietnamese. It was impossible therefore to condemn the heroic armed struggle of the Vietnamese people on pacifist moral grounds. Morality was all on their side.

Another factor that influenced thinking greatly was the waves of violent Black ghetto upheavals that swept the country. The combustible material for these explosions had been accumulating for a long time in the intolerable, humiliating conditions of ghetto oppression. The sparks that set them off were specific acts of police brutality.

Once again it became morally impossible to condemn these outbursts. People who face oppression and violence every day of their lives cannot be expected—should not be expected—to continue taking them. It was then that the issues of self-defense and the right to bear arms in this defense arose as questions of major concern. It was then too that the Student Nonviolent Coordinating Committee began to fade into the background and the newly formed Black Panther Party came to the fore.

2. *Violence as a Moral Question*

THE EXPERIENCES of life itself, therefore, have helped make clear that the question of violence cannot be approached from a purely abstract moral point of view.* The truth is that no one can honestly say that he is opposed to violence under every and all circumstances.

Let us take an extreme hypothetical example. A man suddenly goes beserk, gets a machine gun and begins to mow down children leaving school. Who, under these circumstances, would hesitate to stop him *by whatever means are necessary?* Who would dare to accuse the person who did this selfless act, violent though it be, of immorality? Would it not be the other way around?

The man or woman who saved these young lives at the risk of his own would be worthy of highest respect and praise. But one who failed to act decisively at such a moment of truth, and then sought to excuse this cowardice on moral grounds, would be worthy only of utter contempt.

Although violence cannot be judged from an abstract moral point of view, there is a moral question involved. The violence must be justifiable; not alone to the individual or individuals who employ it—even the madman in our hypothetical example would somehow justify his actions to his own demented mind—but justifiable to others. Not justifiable to the class of oppressors and exploiters, but justifiable to the people.

No sane person wants violence for the sake of violence. Whoever finds pleasure in injury to others is sick, mentally and morally sick. He is a person drained of his humanity. Hence there must be good reason for resorting to violent means of struggle, and the blame for this must be clearly evident as stemming from the actions of the ruling class. Whoever appears to be sanctioning violence for its own sake, will lose the sympathy and support of the people.

In a recent strike of 1,100 meat-packing workers in the Iowa-

---

*"There is a primary violence, the mother of all violence, which is the injustice that exists almost everywhere. . . . There are small groups of privileged families whose riches are maintained by the misery of millions of fellow citizens. I call injustice violence because, in fact, misery kills more than the most bloody wars. Hunger creates physical, psychological and moral distortions." (Brazilian Archbishop Helder P. Camara, *New York Times*, October 28, 1970).

Nebraska region, hundreds of incidents of violence occurred. Tires were slashed, homes and power lines dynamited, men and women beaten. The company, the Iowa Beef Processors, Inc., brought hundreds of scabs into the plant under the protection of the police and company thugs. Whatever acts of violence may have been committed by strikers were minor and insignificant compared to the violence of the company and the police.

Every worker who has ever walked a picket line, been unemployed, or without food for his family, will understand that whatever violence these strikers were compelled to use in defense of their jobs and their livelihood was justifiable, while the violence used by the corporation and police to break the strike was unjustifiable.

When the ghettos erupted in the summer of '66 and '67, only a minority of Black people actually participated in the so-called "rioting," yet the great majority of ghetto residents sympathized with them. They blamed the oppressive racist conditions and the police terror, not the young rebels.

Justifiability is not to be mistaken for legality. Laws are part of the superstructure erected by the exploiting class to institutionalize the protection of its vested property interests. Laws are therefore most frequently unjustifiable because they are meant to maintain class exploitation and national oppression. Justifiability is therefore only a moral issue in a class sense, in a political sense.

From a political point of view violence must also be justified on the ground of expediency. Even when the provocation may be exceedingly great, the gauntlet cannot be picked up every time the class adversary throws it down. Some people do not understand this. Their reaction is purely individualistic and emotional. They are outraged and want to prove their valor—immediately, right now. They do not think what the consequences may be. They fail to realize that they are engaged in a war of the exploited and oppressed against their exploiters, and not in a single act of combat. They are not Davids, who single-handed, with slingshot, are to kill the Goliaths of our day. Neither are they the legendary knights of yore who fought for personal love and glory. They are engaged in a struggle with a powerful and ruthless foe; they are fighting in a war, which like all wars, requires strategy and tactics to be won. Without such an outlook the Movement is game for any trap the other side sets.

The ruling class in this country is quite adept at setting many traps, especially today when it has learned from recent world history what people can accomplish once they organize, unite, and are guided by revolutionary ideals and a revolutionary strategy and tactics.

Sacrifices are inevitable in any struggle; so are mistakes. People respect courage and expect it from those who would lead them. But they have no respect for those who provoke needless and senseless sacrifices. They admire daring, wish to emulate it, but run from folly like the plague. They will not put their fate in the hands of those who are more concerned with bravado than with what is best for the struggle as a whole.

There is still another aspect of this question. It is simplistic to believe that State power rests solely on police guns and soldier's bayonets. In the final analysis it does, i.e., when the ruling class and its State power have lost legitimacy in the eyes of the majority of people. Then the gun takes command. But society cannot live and function balanced on the terror of a bayonet.

Every ruling class and every government is concerned therefore with influencing public opinion, seeks to justify its policies, and endeavors to win a larger degree of popular support for itself. Those people it cannot win over or bribe, it tries to confuse and demoralize so as to neutralize and make them passive. And it always aims to impress people with its own power and durability, to show that opposition is futile, and that the only alternative to itself is the deluge.*

In the United States the illusion that this is a truly democratic country in which the people have the determining voice is widespread. The government can still claim that its legitimacy stems from the popular will. It cannot claim this for every

---

*"We have always known and repeatedly pointed out that the bourgeoisie maintains itself in power *not* only by force but also by virtue of the lack of class-consciousness and organization, the routinism and downtrodden state of the masses" (Lenin, "Letters on Tactics," pp. 46-47).

governmental policy or action—although it tries to do so—but it can make this claim for the character of the rule itself.

The situation here is quite different therefore from that in countries where there are open dictatorships and where the legitimacy of rule is already greatly undermined and constantly under popular challenge.

Bearing this in mind, the tactics of the Movement in this country must aim to expose the true state of affairs, the exploitative class nature of our society and democratic institutions. These tactics must bring to light constantly the ruling-class responsibility for the violence of our times, whether in Vietnam, Harlem, or Berkeley.

The Establishment must never be permitted to get away with its hypocritical pose of being peaceful and democratic. Tactics that appear to shift the responsibility for violence and undemocratic acts to the Movement, are exceedingly harmful and even dangerous, for they not only bolster illusions in the liberality of the system, but legitimize its rule and its right to use even greater repression against opposition.

3. Does Repression Always Expose the System?

THERE IS a mistaken belief in some circles of the new radicalism that increased repression is a good thing, should even be provoked, to expose more easily the oppressive class character of the system.

This is a dangerously mistaken view. Two things are forgotten: First, that a great deal depends upon how the repression comes about; whom the people hold responsible for it. Second, that repression does not lead automatically to greater militancy and resistance. Sometimes it leads to a feeling of hopelessness and despair and therefore to tactics of frustration or complete passivity, which accomplish nothing.

Fascism in Germany did not lead to revolution. It led to the crushing of the working class and revolutionary movements and then to world war. In Italy likewise, fascism remained in power for 22 years and then was overthrown by a combination of internal revolt and allied military invasion. And the problem of revolution in both Italy and West Germany remains unresolved a quarter of a century after the war. In Spain, Franco is still in power after more than 30 years with the aid of U. S. dollars and arms.

There are numerous historical examples to prove that the way people react to violence depends upon whom they blame for it. When Hitler took power in Germany, in January 1933, he did not take it by force of arms. It was handed him "legally" by President Von Hindenburg—the very man elected as the liberal choice to keep Hitler out of power.

Representing at the time a declining minority of voters (the Nazis had lost heavily in the preceding election), Hitler sought legitimacy for his regime in a new national election. To make sure that he would win required the destruction of the opposition and first of all the Communist Party. But this had to be done in such a way as not to boomerang against the regime itself. A way had to be found to make it appear that the Communists were responsible for their own destruction.

The way that was found was the deliberate burning of the Reichstag—the German parliament—and placing the blame on the Communists for this senseless act. A half-wit by the name of Van der Lubbe was lured to the site of the fire, "caught," and made to confess that the Communists were responsible for the arson as the signal for revolution. Georgi Dimitroff, the Bulgarian Communist leader in exile in Germany, and three other Communist leaders were framed up; a national hysteria was created; mass arrests followed; stormtrooper violence swept the streets; the people were bewildered and confused; the opposition was crushed; the elections were "won."*

Why did Hitler, the fascist, whose regime rested on the guns of stormtroopers, police and army, still find it necessary to fabricate so monstrous a frame-up? The answer is clear. He sought to shift the blame for violence to the Communists and the Left and in this way to divide and confuse the masses.

*Actually, Hitler did not win a majority of the vote even then; he won a plurality, about 43 per cent of the total.

Another historic example comes to mind. In St. Petersburg, now Leningrad, in 1905, hundreds of hungry workers, including women and children, marched to the tsar's palace to petition him for bread. The demonstration was led by a priest, Father Gapon—later discovered to have been a police agent—and the petitioners carried their religious crosses and ikons with them. As they peaceably approached the palace the troops were ordered to shoot and hundreds of innocent people were slaughtered.

The purpose of this cold-blooded massacre was simple: it was meant as a warning in the midst of the growing discontent and unrest; it was meant to intimidate and frighten the masses. It accomplished the opposite effect. It did not snuff out the flames of discontent; it fanned them to white hot fury. It showed people how illusory was their hope that the "Little Father" would intervene in their behalf. It marked the dramatic opening scene to the Revolution of 1905.

It is therefore true that ruling class repression can tear the veil from people's eyes and shatter illusions in the character of the system and the regime. But this does not occur when the violence seems to have been provoked and when repression is given popular sanction by individual acts of violence arising from frustration that cannot be distinguished from actions of agent provocateurs.

We can come closer to home for historic examples to prove the same thing. The Haymarket Square frame-up of 1886 is one such incident. A bomb was thrown during a mass meeting of strikers of the McCormick Harvester Works in Chicago, protesting the killing of six strikers a few days before. The strike at the plant was part of a nationwide struggle to win the eight-hour work day. Chicago was the heart and sinew of the effort.

The bomb killed seven policemen and four workers. As a consequence, a nationwide hysteria was whipped up, the strike movement smashed, and the labor movement demoralized and set back for a number of years. The top leaders of the Chicago workers' movement were framed up on a murder rap; four were sent to the gallows, one committed suicide to thwart the hangman, and a number of others were sent to prison. The ruling class had achieved its objectives.

Six years later, when calm had returned, John Altgeld, the new Governor of Illinois, opened a new investigation of the bombing, found the convicted men innocent, and freed those still in jail.*

While frame-ups continue to occur, especially in the United States whose ruling class has been adept at organizing these over the years, the Haymarket frame-up was more easily put over because of certain mistakes made by the workers' leadership. Most of them were German immigrants strongly under the influence of the anarchist-terrorist prophet of the time, Johann Most. They had engaged in a great deal of rhetoric about violence and boasted of the great "liberating force" that dynamite could be. They thought they could frighten the employing class to heed the just demands of the workers. As events showed, they only provided the ruling class with the intemperate words that lent credence to the charge against them, and thus helped bring about their conviction.

All this must be borne in mind today when a section of the new radical movement, small though it be, has suddenly become enamored with the old discredited panacea of individual terror.

In 1901, four years before the outbreak of the Russian Revolution of 1905, a section of intellectual, middle-class and upper-class Russian youth also became intoxicated with individual terror as the "new tactic" by which to liberate old Russia. Lenin, who at the time had already begun his struggle to forge a revolutionary vanguard party that could coordinate and lead the fight against both tsarist absolutism and capitalism, saw in the rise of the new terrorist mood a threat to the further advance of the revolutionary movement.

---

*Albert Parsons, the leader of the doomed men, speaking to the court before being sentenced, charged that the employers had organized the throwing of the bomb "to discredit the eight-hour day movement." A few years after the executions, Judge Gary, the trial judge, admitted that evidence showed that a man by the name of Rudolph Schnaubelt had most likely thrown the bomb. On Aug. 6, 1900, the Chicago *Daily Intelligencer*, in a review of the Haymarket affair, pointed out that all evidence "proved that Rudolph Schnaubelt was the miscreant who threw the bomb." Yet, "at a time when the police were rounding up and imprisoning all anarchists and their sympathizers, Schnaubelt was released twice and allowed to make his escape [to Mexico] without the slightest interference by the police officials in Chicago." Nor was there any attempt to extradite him back to the United States (Foner, pp. 110-11).

"The question of terror is not a new question at all," Lenin reminded those who were arguing—as do some today—that the "historic moment" had presented "a completely new question—the question of terror." Lenin had good reason to know this. His own older brother, Alexander, had been executed in 1887 for an attempt to assassinate the tsar.

To those who called for a "change in tactics," Lenin replied that before one can change tactics it is first necessary to have tactics. "Without a strong organization skilled in waging political struggle under all circumstances and at all times," Lenin pointed out, "there can be no question of that systematic plan of action, illumined by firm principles and steadfastly carried out, which alone is worthy of the name of tactics" (Collected Works, "Where to Begin," p. 18).

Lenin, the revolutionist, the Marxist, did not reject terrorism in principle. The movement is still uncoordinated and weak, admonished Lenin. The great mass of discontented people are still largely unorganized. "We, therefore, declare emphatically," he wrote, "that under the present conditions such a means of struggle is inopportune and unsuitable; that it diverts the most active fighters from their real task, the task which is most important from the standpoint of the interests of the movement as a whole; and that it disorganizes the forces, not of the government, but of the revolution."

What, according to Lenin, was needed above all else was a strong staff of "leaders and organizers." These the Russian movement of that time did not yet have. Under such circumstances, asked Lenin, "Is there not the danger of rupturing the contact between the revolutionary organizations and the disunited masses of the discontented, the protesting, and the disposed to struggle, who are weak precisely because they are disunited? Yet *it is this contact that is the sole guarantee of success.*" [Emphasis added]

"Far be it for us," continued Lenin, "to deny the significance of heroic blows, but it is our duty to sound a vigorous warning against becoming infatuated with terror." Terror can only serve as one of the methods of struggle in a period of decisive assault, but the time had not yet come for that. "At the present moment our slogan cannot be, 'To the Assault,' but has to be, 'Lay siege to the enemy fortress.'" The immediate task, Lenin emphasized, is "not to summon all available forces for the attack right now, but to call for the formation of a revolutionary organization capable of uniting all forces and guiding the movement in actual practice and not in name alone; that is, an organization ready to build up and consolidate the fighting forces suitable for the decisive struggles" (ibid., pp. 19-20).

Such was the advice given by the man who later successfully led the Russian working class to the overthrow of capitalism and the establishment of the first socialist state. And his warning against infatuation with terror was written just four years before the time did come to make the first mass assault on the fortress of tsarism.

In the midst of the revolutionary events of 1905-6, Lenin's stress was different. In an article discussing the development of guerrilla warfare in certain areas of Russia, he took the occasion to expound his views more fully on how Marxists should view the question of forms of struggle. It is the clearest and most precise presentation of the subject in all Marxist literature and deserves to be quoted at considerable length:

In the first place, Marxism differs from all primitive forms of socialism by not binding the movement to any one particular form of struggle. It recognizes the most varied forms of struggle; and it does not "concoct" them, but only generalizes, organizes, gives conscious expression to those forms of struggle of the revolutionary classes which arise of themselves in the course of the movement absolutely hostile to all abstract formulas and to all doctrinaire recipes. Marxism demands an attentive attitude to the mass struggle in progress, which, as the movement develops, as the class consciousness of the masses grows, as economic and political crises become acute, continually gives rise to new and more varied methods of defense and attack. Marxism, therefore, positively does not reject any form of struggle. Under no circumstances does Marxism confine itself to the forms of struggle possible and in existence at the given moment only, recognizing as it does that new forms of struggle, unknown to the participants of the given period, inevitably arise as the given social situation changes. In this respect Marxism learns, if we may so express it, from mass practice, and makes no claim whatever to teach the masses forms of struggle invented by "systematisers" in the seclusion of their studies. . . .

In the second place, Marxism demands an absolute historical examination of the question of the forms of struggle. To treat this question apart from the concrete historical situation betrays a failure to understand the rudiments of dialectical materialism. At different stages of economic evolution, depending on differences in political, national-cultural, living and other conditions, different forms of struggle come to the fore, and become the principal forms of struggle; and in connection with this, the secondary auxiliary forms of struggle undergo change in their turn. To attempt to answer yes or no to the question whether any particular means of struggle should be used, without making a detailed examination of the concrete situation of the given moment at the given stage of its development, means completely to abandon the Marxist position ("Guerrilla Warfare," p. 83-84).

We can see therefore how careful Lenin was not to close the door for all times to any forms of struggle, and not to close it for any specific time without first making a concrete examination of the historic moment and conditions. Yet he did not hestitate to slam the door shut on those who in 1901 advocated individual terror and became enamored with terror.

4. Confrontation and Disruption as Tactics

WHAT ABOUT today?—not somewhere else on the globe, but right here in the United States under the specific conditions we face? Is individual terror justified as a tactic or not?

To arrive at a sound answer to this question requires discarding at the outset any abstract moral considerations. When we see what our ruling class is doing in Vietnam and the ocean of blood flowing there; when we think of the centuries-old oppression, misery and sorrow heaped upon the racial minorities in our land; when we remember the oppressive role of U. S. imperialism in Latin America, Africa, Asia and the rest of the world, surely any measures that would hasten the end of this damnable system would be humane and moral, for no amount of violence needed for ending it could compare in magnitude to that employed to keep it alive.

Nor can we permit emotional, subjective considerations to

sway our judgment. Indignation and anger are powerful subjective elements that stoke the fires of revolt and provide drive for carrying on the struggle. But these cannot determine the nature of the tactics to be used. Nor can impatience and frustration do so, or the search for emotional outlets. Our determination must be based on a cool, unemotional, all-sided evaluation of the consequences of each of our actions with one single objective in mind—how best to advance the revolutionary cause; how best to bring closer the day when we can take U.S. imperialism by the scruff of the neck, for when we do it will be a day of rejoicing everywhere.

Remembering what Lenin wrote in 1901, we must first ask ourselves: Are the people of this country now ready to "assault the fortress?" Or is the problem still one of long-range organizing, uniting, and giving articulation and consciousness to the mass discontent that does exist and is bound to grow? To ask these questions is to answer them. No one can seriously contend that we in the United States today are prepared for the revolutionary storming of the heavens.

If this is so, do we not face a similar danger to that described by Lenin? Is there not the grave danger that revolutionists will become diverted from their main task of organizing and leading masses, thereby rupturing their contact with them "that is the sole guarantee of success?"

Those who today advocate terrorist methods of struggle would not necessarily disagree with our estimate that the people in this country are not ready for revolution. But they would draw from this fact an opposite conclusion. They would say that this is all the more reason that something drastic, something dramatic must be done now, not tomorrow. Nor are they impressed with the argument that this may break contact with the larger mass of the people, for they have no confidence that the larger mass can ever be won for revolutionary change. Having no such confidence they want to shoot the works, even if it be just one giant firecracker.

There are some anarchists who believe that terrorist methods alone can bring effective results. They argue, and with considerable evidence in their support, that the powers that be are deaf to popular protest and that only where this is coupled with some form of disruption, or the threat of disruption, are they compelled to listen.

Every workingman knows that this is true from his own personal experience. Employers give raises and settle grievances not because they listen to reason, but because they always know that the workers can shut the plant down and cut off their profits. Every so often they put this to the test and compel the workers to go on strike, i.e., to disrupt production.

Students have learned the same thing in the recent years of student upsurge. The Urban Research Corporation, an organization formed to provide the Establishment with the facts about urban unrest, published "a study of protest on college campuses in this country during 1969." Analyzing all of the varied types of struggles that took place on the campuses for the first six months of the year, the study noted that at the end of that period "some 69% of all demands presented in all protests remained unsatisfied."

Then comes this revealing conclusion:

The more sustained the protest activities—the greater the success. For example, one-time protests achieved negotiations with the Administration in only 20% of the cases. But protests which lasted at least two days achieved negotiations more than 50% of the time. Strikes and building seizures lasting more than a week achieved negotiations in 70% of the cases.

So it would seem from the statistics that the radical point of view that institutions are unyielding unless threats of disruption are levied turn out to be accurate (emphasis added; *New York Times*, January 14, 1970).

A case in point is what happened at Columbia University in 1968. To prevent a school gymnasium from being built on Morningside Heights—a recreation park area in Harlem—the Black students supported by white students occupied a number of school administration buildings. This action became necessary because of the callous indifference of the college administration to the many petitions and protests asking that another site be chosen, and because the decision had been made to begin immediate excavation.

After days of confrontation, involving increasing support from the Black community and a sympathy strike of the student body, the sit-in was broken by a brutal police assault. But the students had won their main demand—work on the gymnasium ceased. The park was restored to the community.

The lessons from these examples are evident. Disruption and confrontation tactics are inevitable where other means fail to get positive response, whether from corporation, educational institution, or the State. But these must be mass actions in this sense: that they articulate real grievances, set realizable objectives, and win the participation and/or the understanding and sympathy of large masses of people. Under no circumstances can they appear to be the artificially contrived gimmicks of confrontation for the sake of confrontation.

Numerous examples could be cited to show the counter-productive consequences of failure to remember this. The Columbia University sit-in was effective in winning its key demand and in educating people to the role of the university as both a servant of big capital and an institution of oppression in its own right. But when the leadership of Students for a Democratic Society (SDS) at the college took this to mean that it should organize confrontation as a permanent way of life, and sought constant disruption for the sake of disruption, it soon lost sympathy and support and shrank into a sect.

Likewise in respect to strikes. Workers will not support strikes for the sake of strikes. Every strike must have its own concrete realizable objectives. The idea of a permanent strike is only an anarchist pipe dream. A worker must work if he is to eat and even the drop-out who refuses to work as "a matter of principle," can only do so by sponging on others as a matter of principle.

The notion of creating confrontation and disruption for the sake of confrontation and disruption is not identical, of course, with that of individual terror. Yet it is a slippery slide that leads nowhere else. It is a tactic so utterly tactless that frustration is its only product. Yet those who use it are so blind that they mistake their own foolishness for that of the masses. Thus, losing confidence in ever being able to win masses, everything seems to depend upon what they themselves will do. As single individuals and small groups can accomplish little without mass support, a stick of dynamite may help them at least sound big. One thing for sure, with it they cannot be ignored. They are important!*

To throw a bomb at a bank, to burn down a building, to break plate-glass windows without cause, is not to conduct revolutionary activity but to play at it; it is "revolution for the hell of it." It does not raise revolutionary class consciousness, does not hurt the war effort or cripple the system, despite hallucinations to the contrary.

It is self-defeating because it creates sympathy for those who deserve none; is meaningless for it accomplishes nothing; and only diverts those who should know better from doing the less romantic, but the essential, slow, difficult work of reaching people, organizing them, and building with them a solid movement of struggle.

Sooner or later it ends up in tragedy. Innocent people get hurt, even if by accident, or the stage is set for another monstrous frame-up, such as were the Haymarket, Mooney-Billings, and Sacco-Vanzetti cases.

There are those, however, who actually believe that the system can be set reeling by terrorist acts. They believe that the high complexity and centralization of modern technology make society more vulnerable to disruption than in the past. Assuming this to be the case, what still is to be accomplished?

Is anyone fool enough to believe that the ruling class is incapable of protecting vulnerable points from *individual* or *grouplet* assaults? And what about the revolution in the technology of communication, of tapped wires, bugged rooms, and agent provocateurs masquerading as the most militant of the most militant and demanding revolutionary action not tomorrow but even sooner than now?

---

*In *The Anarchist Cookbook* there appears this gem: "The actual application of explosives can be a really thrilling and satisfying experience. I have a friend . . . who has told me on several occasions that an explosion for him has an experience very similar to a sexual orgasm. This may seem strange . . . but in many regards is absolutely true" (Powell, p. 112).

Every recent arrest on a terrorist charge has uncovered at least one government agent who led in the wild talk and the formulation of fantastic plans.* What the young terrorists are doing is making it easier for the FBI and CIA to murder Movement people under circumstances in which there is such widespread confusion that no one can prove that the victims themselves were not responsible for their own deaths.† They are also making it easier for innocent people to be framed up on terrorist charges. What a field day this can be for those who wish to destroy the Movement root and branch!‡

Sanction for individual terrorist acts cannot be limited in scope; it sets its own limits that are limitless. Employing these methods as the "answer" to the struggle against the ruling powers, they soon enough become the "answer" to the struggle within the Movement itself between contending ideological currents and political tendencies. In Los Angeles this led to the

---

*We shall cite one example out of many. In 1965, Robert Collier and two others were arrested and charged with plotting to blow up the Statue of Liberty. A fourth member of the group turned out to be an undercover police agent. It was he who used police funds to pay for the dynamite and to rent the car to pick it up. He had masterminded the whole plot (Kempton, 1970).

†It is still to be learned who blew up Ralph Featherstone and a companion in Maryland. The police insist that the deaths were the result of an accident, but his friends and associates insist that this young Black leader had nothing to do with dynamite and that it must have been planted in his car.

‡Since these lines were written some changes have taken place. The death of three of their comrades in the New York City Eleventh Street townhouse explosion of March 1970, has resulted in some Weatherman soul searching. In a new public statement issued in December 1970, the Weatherpeople, as they now call themselves, believe that their single stress on "bombings and picking up the gun" was a "military error." They now stress that it is also necessary to build a mass movement. But they see the possibility for such a movement only among the young people in the counter-culture communities. Here is where they think the action is and where a "New Nation" will "grow out of the struggles of the next year." While their admission that the bombings of the past two years have been counter-productive is important, as it may bring a more basic rethinking, such a more fundamental approach is not yet forthcoming. To build hopes on the quicksand of the "do-your-own thing" life style "revolution," is to invite more frustration and disillusion. A more complete break with anarchist individualism and elitism is necessary. But this can come only when there is recognition that it is the great mass of ordinary people, and first of all the working class, upon which the revolutionary movement must be based.

killing of two members of the Black Panther Party by a few members of a contending black cultural-nationalist organization. In New York City, one group of employees of the *Guardian,* the radical newsweekly, with the help of anarchist friends, physically stormed and occupied *Guardian* premises, ousted members of the paper's staff, and "liberated" it.

Unless methods of struggle of this kind within the Movement are rapidly and decisively put to an end they may set the Movement back for a long period of time. It must become an inflexible law within the Movement that force and violence can never be used to settle internal disputes. The law of the Mafia and the CIA cannot be permitted to operate within the Movement.

This does not require toning down disagreements over ideology and policy. But the purpose must be to build the Movement, not to destroy it. Anyone who forgets this, who introduces into the Movement the gangster tactics of violence and disruption, must be treated as an enemy, for he is that whether conscious of it or not. Once again, anarcho-terrorist methods can only make it easier for the hand of the enemy, masquerading as the hand of a friend, to pull the trigger.

This tendency to use violence and disruption within the Movement is not something new in the history of anarchism. In 1869, a Russian disciple and close associate of Michael Bakunin, a man by the name of Sergei Nechayev, published a *Catechism of Revolution* which became something of a handbook for terrorists everywhere. In this *Catechism* he defended the right and duty of revolutionists to operate without scruples whatsoever. He urged lying, stealing, entering into "suitable relations with prostitutes, with the police, with 'the so-called criminals,' etc." The guiding purpose of the secret conspiratorial organization he favored was "to increase existing evils in order that people may lose patience and may be stimulated to a mass rising."*

In that same year he helped form a conspiratorial society

---

*It is not certain whether Nechayev wrote the *Catechism.* "Many regarded the *Catechism* as the work of Bakunin who never denied the supposition." It was also reprinted in Drogomanov's edition of *Bakunin's Correspondence.* (Masaryk, p. 470).

among Moscow students. One of the first acts was the assassination of a fellow student accused of treason because he had begun to doubt some of the claims made by Nechayev. An "additional reason for this bloodletting" is that Nechayev "desired to intimidate his own followers, to knit them more closely together, and to promote and spread the idea of pandestruction by the excitement which the murder would cause" (Masaryk, pp 471-72).

Both Bakunin and Nechayev were accused by the General Council of the First International, headed by Karl Marx, "of having sent innocent persons to their doom in Russia" by exposing them to the police.

After his exposure Nechayev admitted the real state of affairs. He acknowledged openly and with the utmost impudence that it was his custom to compromise deliberately those who were not completely in agreement with him in order either to destroy them or to draw them into the movement completely. In accordance with the same reprehensible principles he would persuade people to sign compromising declarations in a moment of excitement, or he would steal compromising letters in order afterward to be able to exercise extortionate pressure on their authors (Mehring, p. 464).

Referring to these nefarious activities of Nechayev, Engels wrote: "How far the Russian police is involved in this I shall leave as a moot question for the present . . . *Nechayev is either a Russian agent provocateur* or, anyhow, acted as if he were" ("Anarchism and Conspiratorial Ethics," p. 445).*

5. Heroic Acts to Stop the War

IN REFERRING to this tendency of anarchism, and in the first place its terrorist wing, to create a situation of disintegrating chaos in which it is difficult to distinguish friend from foe, we do not wish to impugn the motives of most of the young people who have become enchanted with terrorist romanticism. Many of them

---

*"I fell in love with Bakunin and Nechayev's *Catechism of the Revolutionist.* I took the *Catechism* for my bible and. . . I began consciously incorporating these principles in my daily life, to employ tactics of ruthlessness in my dealings with everyone with whom I came into contact" (Eldridge Cleaver, *Soul on Ice*, p. 25).

have fallen under this spell with the very finest of motives. They see the war in Vietnam continuing despite all that the mass movement has done to try to stop it. They feel that blow must be struck against blow. In the face of the wholesale bloodletting being perpetrated by American imperialism in Vietnam they believe that ordinary methods of protest are not enough and that everything should be done to try to stop it.

We deeply respect these feelings and we share them. These are not ordinary times, and ordinary methods of struggle are *not* enough. But neither can gestures—not even wild gesticulations—provide a substitute. Whatever we do must have a purpose, an objective, must fit into a strategy. We cannot help the Vietnamese if we play into the hands of imperialism. We cannot help end the war if it is made easier for the ruling class to smash the Movement. We cannot bring the boys home if the mass movement against the war declines, if people become demoralized, if the fight is narrowed down to the actions of a handful of individuals, self-sacrificing and heroic though they may be.

There must be more, not less, bold and heroic acts against the war, both individual and mass. But these must serve a purpose. They must help focus greater public attention on the war, further clarify the issues involved, and not permit the discussion to be sidetracked and diverted into irrelevant channels. The result must be ever greater revulsion to the war, ever greater activity against it, and ever greater difficulties for its prosecution.

We are all for the heroic acts of young people in resisting the draft or in refusing to go to fight in Vietnam. If GIs acted to stop the war machine, if longshoremen refused to load arms ships, if seamen refused to sail them, if workers refused to produce planes, tanks and munitions, these would be meaningful acts of heroism understandable by all and would indeed mark a decisive turning point in the war.

We can understand why some people are tired of repeating the same kind of protest demonstrations against the war. But we reject the view that these actions do no good. It is generally acknowledged that a majority of the people want an end to the war. The mighty mass demonstrations against it have certainly contributed toward this, showing people that they were not alone in their doubts or opposition. Even the fact that Nixon is compelled to promise the withdrawal of more men from Vietnam, no matter what his intentions may be, is an indication of how he fears public opinion and desires to placate it. And to the extent that he reneges on his promises it is possible to arouse even more people against the war, against the Administration, and against the system responsible for it.

Since the large-scale military invasion of Vietnam began in 1965, a peace movement has developed in this country in some ways more massive and militant than anywhere else in the world, and with growing anti-imperialist consciousness. To think this is nothing, has accomplished nothing, is to make a tragic error of judgment.

The big task is to spread and build this movement, especially among the workers. They feel the economic effects of the war and more and more are becoming increasingly restive under them. It is now possible to make the war an issue of debate and action within the labor movement, and to show the direct relationship between inflation, high taxes, poor housing, pollution and urban decay, and the cost of militarism and war. The increasingly youthful composition of the labor movement also is a positive factor, for the young have been against this war more than any other age bracket.

When the first shop, plant, mine, mill, ship or dock closes down in protest against the war—even if only for a day—this will add an ingredient to the anti-war movement a thousand times more effective than the hit-and-run tactics of smashing windows or throwing bombs.

6. Guerrilla Warfare

A MISREADING of current world history has contributed to lending credence to the mistaken view that small handfuls of intrepid individuals can somehow replace the masses in the making of revolution.

In Cuba, a small courageous group led by Fidel Castro did start the guerrilla war. But what is forgotten is that it had the sympathy of the great majority of the people and the active aid of the peasantry in the agrarian areas of guerrilla combat. What is also forgotten is the relatively high level of consciousness among the workers, the result of decades of Communist work and influence. Without this, the small band could not have survived a fortnight, let alone grown into a mighty liberating force.

The Batista regime was a brutal, oppressive, armed dictatorship. It served the interests of American imperialism and its Cuban lackeys. Its stable of venal, corrupt, bootlicking politicians only further enhanced its general unpopularity. What was needed under the circumstances was not just exposure of the regime, for it already stood naked in the public eye. What was needed was to show the masses how the military dictatorship could be overthrown by the only means that could do so—armed combat. This Castro did. History attests to the correctness of his judgment and his action.

But where a regime still has legitimacy in the eyes of the people, where it appears to be ruling by popular mandate, armed struggle—whether the guerrilla or the individual terrorist kind—cannot bring about revolution, only its reverse.

Che Guevara, in an article, "Lessons of the Cuban Revolution," made this point crystal clear. He sharply castigated those who believe "that against a professional army nothing can be done, who sit down to wait until in some mechanical way all necessary objective and subjective conditions are given [for revolution] without working to accelerate them."

But he did not stop there. He went on to point out that "a necessary minimum" of conditions is required, without which success is impossible. "People must see clearly the futility of maintaining the fight for social goals within the framework of civil debate," he wrote, and added: "Where a government has come to power through some form of popular vote, fraudulent or not, and maintains at least an appearance of constitutional legality, the guerrilla outbreak cannot be promoted, since the possibilities of peaceful struggle have not yet been exhausted" (Guevara, pp. 287-88).

Whether failure to remember this was a factor that led to the Bolivian tragedy in which this brilliant, heroic revolutionary leader gave his life, history will have to judge. As for the United States, the meaning of Che's words is self-evident. We can neither sit back and wait passively for things to change, nor can we adopt forms and methods of struggle for which a necessary minimum of conditions do not exist. In the United States there is no military dictatorship, the government has come to power by popular vote, and the possibilities of peaceful struggle have not yet been exhausted. This is not to say that the growth of repression will not change this situation.

It is also necessary to say something about Mao's slogan, "All power grows through the barrel of a gun." If by this catchphrase is meant that victory in armed combat is determined by armed means, or that State power when defended by arms must be vanquished by arms, these are somewhat oversimplified generalizations, but we can let them pass. But the slogan has been popularized and used in another way that is extremely harmful.

Guns are seen as the great liberator. But guns do not make revolutions; people do. To glorify guns, to stress and overstress them, is to make oneself a prisoner of rhetoric that becomes a roadblock to reaching and organizing people. Sometimes it is even seen as an alternative to this. Also it enables the ruling class to frighten masses with the specter of armed violence coming from the Left, enabling it thereby to get away more easily with its own murderous assaults, especially on young Black radicals.

Speaking of this problem, Gus Hall, General Secretary of the Communist Party, has noted that whether or when to use guns is not a question of principle, but of tactics. "It seems to me that whether the people have guns in their homes is not the issue. I think most Americans do. Also, the right to self-defense is not the issue here. As police brutality increases, the right of self-defense will grow in importance. But the advocacy of the slogan, 'Pick up the gun,' is another matter." What would be the result of such a tactical slogan? he asks. Would it get mass response? Would it in fact result in self defense? "I do not think so. It would result only in individual actions, if any," and it would "alienate" larger masses "who are moving into struggle" ("Speech to Young Workers' Liberation League," February 1970).

The big job, whether in the ghettos or elsewhere, is to help the people to organize themselves, to give direction to their struggle and to develop leadership. This must include the right of armed self-defense against police or racist violence, and the organization of *mass* self-defense by a variety of means.

Another influence that has served to feed terrorist thinking has been the impact of the movie, "The Battle of Algiers." This dealt with organized terrorist acts within the city of Algiers during the Algerian war for national liberation from French rule.

An attempt has been made to mechanically transpose the conditions of Algeria to the United States, and to see the Black and minority peoples as playing the role of the Algerian guerrillas with the support of white revolutionists.

There is something terribly wrong in this comparison. In the first place, the movie itself distorts the actual situation. It never shows the terrorist acts in the city of Algiers as part of a national war of liberation in which guerrilla armies were fighting the French army in the countryside. Secondly, the terrorist activities in the city of Algiers had as their purpose the creation of conditions in which the French would have to leave the country, no longer able to live, function, or continue to make profit in it.

But in Algeria nine-tenths of the population was native and only one-tenth was French colonialist. It was possible to drive the French minority out, but is there anyone crazy enough to suggest that the objective of Black liberation is to drive the white majority out of this country? Furthermore, in Algeria the working class was nearly all native; in the United States it is Black, Brown and white.

In the United States, unlike Algiers, the system cannot be overthrown by the Black, Brown and other minority peoples alone. It can be done only by the working class as a whole.

Any viewing of the Algiers struggle as a model for the United States could only mean a race war. The white ruling class would be the gainer and the struggle of both the Black people and the working class would be set back for generations.

There is something reprehensible in this attempt of some confused white young terrorists to put the Black people in the role of the Algerians. It is to ask the Black people to make the revolution for all of us, which from the point of view of this writer smells of racism. Henry Winston was certainly correct when he stated that armed uprisings "cannot be successful by the black communities alone, no matter how courageous they struggle" ("Unity and Militancy for Freedom and Equality." p. 5).

Nor should those who romanticize the Algerian struggle forget one truth that the movie did bring out: the terrorist organization in Algiers was infiltrated by the police; its members were all caught and executed.

In the ranks of young radicals there is a great deal of admiration for the way in which the Vietnamese people have astounded the world with their ability to fight and to win against a power that seemed militarily invincible. But what they fail to see is that this "miracle" is the product of many years of tireless work and could not have been possible without winning the support of and drawing the people themselves into the struggle.

There is no other way, *anywhere!!*

CHAPTER VII

IN SEARCH OF AN AGENCY

1. The "Revolution Now" Pessimists

STRANGE AS it may seem, many of those who shout the loudest for "revolution *now*", have no perspective for revolution at any time. They really do not believe that a broad-based, deep-rooted and growing movement for revolutionary change is possible in this country. It is a case of rhetoric used to conceal a lack of analysis and program.

The literature of the new radicalism is sprinkled with pessimism about the possibility of building a mass movement, especially among working people. It is filled with the belief that the capitalist economic system has somehow, willy-nilly been able to resolve all its internal contradictions.

Paul Goodman, for example, is one of those who strongly detest the system for what it does to the individual. But what he finds wrong with the system is not, "as the socialists predicted, that it doesn't work, but that it works splendidly." What he means by "splendidly" is that it seems to be foolproof. He points to the phoniness of the "pluralism" liberals swear by. He notes that the various centralized bureaucracies interlock so that, "Conflict becomes coalition, harmony becomes consensus, and the social machine runs with no checks at all" (pp. 128-29). Hence Goodman does not like the *way* the system works because it works its diabolical way so "splendidly."

Theodore Roszak, in his *Making of a Counter Culture,* says that those who gamble on capitalism's incapacity finally to eliminate material poverty and gross physical exploitation "are making a risky wager." "It is certainly one of the oldest, but one of the weakest radical arguments which insists stubbornly that capitalism is *inherently* incapable of laying golden eggs for everyone" (pp. 9-10). He admits that "there are those who have not yet been cut in on the material advantages," and even foresees "a forceful indignant campaign" to bring the excluded into "general affluence." This may prove to be an exhausting struggle, he concedes, but at the end of it—"why should we doubt it?"—all the disadvantaged minorities will be accommodated. So sure is he of this that he warns, "It might even be a trick . . . like the ruse of someone you wish to capture to lean all his weight on a door you hold closed—and then, all of a sudden, throw it open. He not only winds up inside, where you want him, but he comes crashing in full tilt" (pp. 113-14).

According to Roszak, therefore, if the Black, the Chicano, the Puerto Rican and Indian people have not gotten their just share yet—assuming that all whites do have it, which, of course, is far from the case*—there is nothing to really worry about. It is all a matter of good time.

2. Marcuse As Revolutionary Guru

THE MAIN radical theorist of the view that modern technological society can and does meet the material needs of its people is Herbert Marcuse. He argues that modern capitalism has tremendous "absorbent power" through its capacity to provide material satisfaction "in a way which generates submission and weakens the rationality of protest." Thus for him too the economic system seems to be working diabolically well. The only fly in the ointment is the way the system uses the growing, spreading abundance to generate submission and to weaken protest.

In his book, *One-Dimensional Man,* Marcuse writes: "Technological progress, extended to a whole system of domination and coordination, creates forms of life (and of power) which appear to reconcile the forces opposing the system and to defeat or refute all protest in the name of the historical prospects of freedom from toil and domination."

*According to official government figures it is estimated that there are some 35 million people in the United States living in conditions of poverty; 20 million of these are whites.

"Contemporary society," continues Marcuse, "seems to be capable of containing social change—qualitative change which could establish essentially different institutions, a new direction of the productive process, new modes of human existence." And to make sure we do not miss the point, he adds: "This containment of social change is perhaps the most singular achievement of advanced industrial society . . ." (pp. x, xi).

Marcuse is saying, in other words, that the system is capable of preventing revolution. That it has been capable of doing so thus far is self evident. But if this is true for the future as well, and this is what Marcuse is saying, then there is no hope for a bonafide revolutionary movement in the United States and hence no sense in trying to build one. If Marcuse is right, capitalism has indeed discovered the secret of eternal life.

It seems strange, therefore, that so many young people who consider themselves dyed-in-the-wool r-r-revolutionists should have viewed Marcuse as the very guru of revolution. Although his fame as the septuagenarian prophet of the "New Left" declined in the last few years, it is still remarkable that it lasted so long.

There is good reason why his ideas struck a responsive chord. They addressed themselves to new features of social development and gave the appearance of basic answers to new problems. In Marcuse's description of modern capitalist society many middle-class white youth saw a reflection of their own particular reality. These young people were in the main the sons and daughters of "the affluent society." They came from homes to which the postwar years and the new technology had brought considerable well-being. But greater material possessions had meant neither greater happiness nor had it increased their sense of security or community.

The revolt of middle-class white youth was not against material lack; it was against spiritual void. They felt loathing for society's stress on material possessions in direct proportion to their ability to have them. They were, after all, what Paul Goodman with good reason called the new breed of aristocrats, "the first generation in America selective of the standard of living." Thus Marcuse's attack on "consumerism" as the vise by which the ruling class puts the squeeze on individuals and makes the working class impotent, found ready response among these young people. It fed both their dislike for the system and their elitist feelings of superiority to the working class.* By shifting the concept of oppression from the arena of production relations to that of consumption, the men and women who work to meet their material needs are downgraded, while the nonworking and non-producing strata are upgraded.

Behind this elitism lurks a hidden unspoken fear that new technological changes gradually are undermining former middle-class insularity and independence. These changes are turning everyone but the very rich into wage or salaried cogs of a working class that is new only in the sense that it now includes many new categories of mental labor. As has been suggested by others, previous college generations were "pre-bourgeois;" this one is "pre-working class."

Marx and Engels noted that when the old order begins to crumble "a portion of the bourgeoisie goes over to the proletariat, and in particular, a portion of the bourgeois ideologists, who have raised themselves to the level of comprehending theoretically the historical movement as a whole." But Marx and Engels noted also another phenomenon—that many of the lower middle classes come to the revolution for essentially conservative reasons, "in view of their impending transfer into the proletariat" (*Communist Manifesto*, p. 19).

Both of these tendencies are at work today as the crisis of the system deepens. The latter tendency assumes mass proportions and frequently exhibits itself in a confusing and contradictory fashion. There is at one and the same time an impassioned hatred for the system and yet an even tighter clinging to certain elitist, individualist, middle-class concepts and prejudices.

In some ways Marcuse became the theoretical expression *par*

---

*This point is made exceedingly well by Ellen Willis in an article, "Consumerism and Women." She writes: "This elitism is evident in radicals' convictions that they have seen through the system, while the average working slob is brain-washed." Then, tongue-in-cheek, she observes: "Oddly, no one claims that the ruling class is oppressed by commodities; it seems that rich people consume out of free choice" (Willis, p. 80).

excellence of this ambivalence. He had an important and beneficial impact on the "New Left" for a period of time, introducing it to a serious, even if incorrect, discussion of Marxist philosophy, theory and practice. This was an important factor in breaking youth from their passionately held non-ideological views of the early Sixties. Furthermore, some of his writings also contain brilliant insights into the insanities and irrationalities of American society. At the same time his theories tended to reinforce the elitist prejudices that middle-class youth absorbed from their surroundings, especially their disdain for merging with the plebeian mass of the working class. Marcuse acknowledges that the bourgeoisie and the working class "are still the basic classes" of our society. But he contends that capitalist technological development "has altered the structure and function of these two classes in such a way that they no longer appear to be the agents of historical transformation." There is now "an absence of demonstrable agents and agencies of social change" (p. xiii).

While Marcuse is quite sure that the system can now contain qualitative social change and that there is an absence of agencies of social change, he is not always absolutely sure of this. He confesses to a certain ambiguity and ambivalence. He vacillates between "two contradictory hypotheses: 1) that advanced society is capable of containing qualitative change for the foreseeable future; 2) that forces and tendencies exist which may break this containment and explode society" (p. xv). Of one thing he seems certain: the containment will not be broken by the working class.* His only hope lies in what he calls the "substratum"—the "outsiders and the poor, the unemployed and unemployable, the persecuted colored races, the inmates of prisons and mental institutions" (*ibid.*, p. 53).

---

*Following the May-June 1968 events in France, Marcuse became less certain of this. He began to see the possibility of a revolutionary potential for the working class in the developed capitalist countries. Yet he has never departed from his basic analysis in *One-Dimensional Man.* On the one hand he writes, "Today the classical contradictions within capitalism are stronger than they have ever been before" ("On Utopia," *Ramparts,* April 1970). Yet when he spells out these contradictions he does not even mention the class contradiction!

By "substratum" Marcuse means the lumpenproletariat. But the poor, the unemployed, the great majority of the oppressed minority peoples, and many of those in prison, are part of the working class. To see the working class as composed only of those who have jobs, or only of those in the higher wage brackets, or only of whites, is to create a working class out of one's prejudices, not as it really is.

But even after creating a "substratum" of the most exploited and oppressed of the working class, Marcuse is not optimistic of what it can accomplish. "Nothing indicates that it will be a good end." The resources of the "established societies are sufficiently vast to allow for adjustments and concessions to the under dog, and their armed forces sufficiently trained and equipped to take care of emergency situations."

Thus, after finding a new social agency for revolutionary change in the "substratum," Marcuse still has doubts. It is not surprising that he winds up his book on a dismal note and with a somber quote: "It is only for the sake of those without hope that hope is given to us" (pp. 256-7).

3. From Bakunin to Eldridge Cleaver

MARCUSE IS by no means alone in turning wistful eyes to the lumpenproletariat in the hope that it will be the stratum to make the revolution. A whole literature now exists on the subject. While the view that the lumpenproletariat is now the truly revolutionary class is something of a current fad in sections of the new radicalism, it is not new. Bakunin made this a major point of difference with Marxism. He insisted that the lumpenpropletariat was the *real* proletariat.

Because so many seem to think this is some new theory arising out of present-day conditions alone, it is worth reminding ourselves what Bakunin said on this matter nearly a century ago:

By the flower of the proletariat I mean precisely that eternal "meat for governments, that great *rabble of the people* ordinarily designated by Messrs. Marx and Engels by the phrase at once picturesque and contemptuous of "*lumpenproletariat*," the "riff-raff," that rabble which, being very nearly unpolluted by all bourgeois civilizations carries in its heart, in its aspirations, in all the necessities and miseries of its collectivist position, all the germs of the Socialism of the future, and which alone is powerful enough today to inaugurate the Social Revolution and bring it to triumph (Bakunin, p. 38).

As history has since shown, the lumpenproletariat did not inaugurate or bring a socialist revolution to triumph, neither in Russia, Bakunin's homeland, nor anywhere else in the world. In every *socialist* revolution that has taken place to date, it was the working class that carried the revolution to triumph in alliance with the poor peasants, sections of the lower middle class, and a portion of the intellectuals and lumpenproletariat.

This, of course, does not answer the question for our day. Things may have changed so, or be so different in the United States, that past precedents do not hold. There are some people who think they do not. They differ from Bakunin's view in only one respect: he openly challenged Marxism while they claim to be applying Marxism creatively. They claim to be Marxists-Leninists.

Eldridge Cleaver is one such theorist. He wrote a special article which was reprinted as a pamphlet dealing with this single question. In it he opens a broadside against those Marxist-Leninists who like flunkies, in his belief, are slavishly adhering to what Marx wrote about the lumpenproletariat a century ago. He believes that Marx and Engels, for all their great contributions to socialist thought, "were themselves racists." Furthermore, "Historically, Marxism-Leninism has been an outgrowth of European problems and it has been primarily preoccupied with finding solutions to European problems." Here, he argues, racism has made the difference. "White workers belong to a totally different world than that of Black workers." Yet he concludes that both white and Black workers make up the "Right wing of the Proletariat," while "the lumpenproletariat is the Left-Wing." The lumpenproletariat is therefore the revolutionary stratum of the proletariat and destined to lead the revolution. The Black Panther Party is the proud spokesman and representative of the Black lumpenproletariat. This is Cleaver's thesis. He puts it this way:

O.K. We are lumpen. Right on. The Lumpenproletariat are all those who have no secure relationship or vested interests in the means of production and the institutions of capitalist society. That part of the "Industrial Reserve Army" held perpetually in reserve; who have never worked and never will; who can't find a job; who are unskilled and unfit; who have been displaced by machines, automation, and cybernation, and were never "retrained and invested with new skills," all those on Welfare or receiving State aid.

Also the so-called "Criminal Element," those who live by their wits, existing off that which they rip off, who stick guns in the faces of businessmen and say "stick 'em up," or "give it up!" Those who don't even want a job, who hate to work and can't relate to punching some pig's time clock, who would rather punch a pig in the mouth and rob him than punch that same pig's time clock and work for him, those whom Huey P. Newton calls the "illegitimate capitalists." In short, all those who simply have been locked out of the economy and robbed of their rightful social heritage (Cleaver, 1970).

It seems that in each period in which the working class has been slow in coming to class consciousness, and especially when the official labor movement is opportunist-led and reformist-minded, there is an intellectual propensity to look elsewhere, particularly to the intellectuals and lumpenproletariat, as the agency for revolutionary transformation. There is a certain logic in choosing the lumpenproletariat. Who is better qualified to lead and make a revolution than those of the very lowest stratum of society, the outcasts and pariahs, the humans living under the most abject and inhuman conditions? But each society is not just a body of laws and a State power to enforce them; it is in the first place a particular *economic* system of production and exchange. Only that class which can effectuate a revolutionary transformation in the economic base of society can successfully lead and effectuate the revolution. But we are running ahead of our story.

The decay of every former class society brought with it a wholesale dislodgement of people and a growth in absolute misery in a large "unwanted" mass of the population. And this took place side by side with, and was the corollary of, an even more ostentatious, brazen display of wealth, privilege and self-indulgence among the upper classes. The breakdown of feudalism forced millions of peasants off the lands their forefathers had tilled for generations. It set them adrift, roaming from town to town; hungry, ragged, diseased, persecuted; subsisting on what they could and how they could. "Pauperism grew to the proportions of a social crisis. Evicted tenants, jobless journeymen, demobilized soldiers, roamed the highways or littered the slums, begging and robbing to live. In Augsburg, the paupers reckoned at a sixth of the population, in Hamburg a fifth, in London a fourth" (Durant, p. 764).

But despite their large numbers and their terribly wretched conditions of life, the lumpens neither led nor carried to victory the rebellions against feudal society. They fought on both sides of the struggle, some on the side of the princes and others on the side of the people. But even when fighting on the revolutionary side their influence tended to be a demoralizing one. (*See* Engels, *Peasant War in Germany*, p. 45.)

4. The Lumpen Stratum Today

As we have said earlier, past precedent is not enough as an answer to today's problems. It is necessary therefore to consider Eldridge Cleaver's arguments. In the first place it should be recognized that something new has been happening to give a certain underpinning to the belief that the lumpenproletariat is today's agency for revolutionary change. The new scientific-technological revolution—by no means over—has been reducing the percentage of manual workers in the work force, particularly unskilled workers. At the same time technological changes in agriculture are driving more and more people off the land and herding them into the overcrowded central cities. A large percentage of these are Black and Brown people, and an increasing number are not only unemployed but, under present conditions, unemployable. They make up what has become known as the "hard core" unemployed. The rise in the number of people on welfare attests to the seriousness of this problem.*

---

*In June 1969, there were about 9.5 million people receiving federally aided public assistance. Of these, 6.6 million persons were on AFDC (Aid to Families with Dependent Children). In 1967, 48.1 per cent of people on AFDC were non-white (Official reports of the United States Department of Health, Education and Welfare).

The lumpen of the Peasant Wars period described by Engels, and of England and Western Europe *prior* to the industrial revolution, were cast off by a decaying feudal system *before* early manufacturing could absorb them. They could not yet become wage-slaves, even if they wanted to. Marx referred to them as the "fathers of the present working class" who "were chastised for their enforced transformation into vagabonds and paupers" (*Capital*, I, p. 734).

Today's situation is quite different. It arises from the effects of a highly concentrated, technologically developed capitalism. It is also quite different from the situation faced by past generations of European immigrants. These came here when rapidly expanding industrial production could absorb them. Even when unemployed for stretches of time, they were not unemployable. Not so with the Black and Brown people living in the over-crowded rat-infested ghettos of today. Some of them have lived from one generation to the next on public assistance. Even when employed, they are most often underemployed, and so underpaid that their income is not too much greater than those on welfare. Moreover the rapid inroads of a new technology have created a new fear for parents—that their children may have even less opportunity for decent employment than they. It is this that explains the troubled concern with the state of ghetto schools and the rising cry for quality education. But the recent trend toward a saturation of the labor market for educated and trained personnel as well, is adding still another fear, that even increased educational opportunities may not mean increased work opportunities for the great majority.*

Another factor which gives weight to Cleaver's position is the Black revolt which has been transformed from a concern with civil rights to a radical ghetto concern with liberation. The young Black ghetto generation is the heart and soul of this upheaval. Black youth recognize that they have nowhere else to go but to

---

*"The predictable results of motivating non-white welfare clients to complete training courses when employment opportunities are extremely restricted is, for the majority, to produce increased feelings of relative deprivation" (Taylor). "Feelings of relative deprivation" is nice social work language. More aptly said, it would produce increased feelings of anger and outrage.

rebellion. The only question is: What form should it take? Should it be individualistic, self-destructive, anti-social, or should it be organized, disciplined, with conscious revolutionary goals and with both short and long range objectives?

The strong rhetoric and harsh language used, the do-or-die mood, are indicative of the closed-in feeling of desperation that is shared by so many young Blacks today. In 1966, when the official unemployment rate for the country was 3.8 per cent of the labor force, the official rate of joblessness for non-white youth between 16 and 19 years of age was 26.5 per cent. (Private surveys indicated it was even higher than that.) Of 583,000 Black youth between 16 and 24 years of age estimated to be living in the ghettos of our "central cities," 131,000, or 22.5 per cent, were unemployed and from two to three times this number were underemployed (Official government statistics cited in *Report of the President's Commission on National Disorders,* 1968).

Under such circumstances it is not surprising that many Black youth are compelled to live by their wits, to rob, to hustle, to scrounge for the things they need and want. Nor is it strange that these acts of petty crime should appear in their own eyes as acts of individual rebellion, as means by which to strike out at their oppressors, as ways to "liberate" a little of the "loot" being stolen from them by the system of white racist oppression.*

The police who patrol the ghettos, like the occupying army they are, inevitably come into increasing collision with rising young black militancy. Police have murdered Black, with impunity for so long that the very talk of organized resistance, and the measures of armed self-defense that revolutionary Black youth have taken, have further increased police rage and fury. Black youth are seen as the enemy and any outward sign of their determination to be free is considered the greatest of all crimes. Thus Black youth are stopped and humiliated at every opportunity and thrown into prison even without cause.

---

*"The earliest, crudest and least fruitful form of this rebellion (of the workers) was that of crime. . . . Theft was the most primitive form of protest, and for this reason, if for no other, it never became the universal expression of the public opinion of the working-men, however much they might approve of it in silence" (Engels, *The Condition of the Working-Class in England,* pp. 247-48).

It is in such context that the word "pig" has taken on a new generic meaning and the "pigs" are seen as enemy number one—the hated symbol of white oppressive authority and terror.

The slogan "Seize the time!" and the growing number of heroic youth who have been wantonly murdered in the very prime of their lives; the young men and women on trial; the prisons bursting with Black and Brown youth; all, speak to the feelings of desperation that stoke the fires of ghetto rebellion.

It is to the credit of Huey Newton, Bobby Seale and others that they have fought to imbue Black youth with revolutionary consciousness. They have branded the imperialist white ruling class, not all whites, as the oppressor. They have recognized that liberation is impossible under capitalism and that the ultimate goal must be socialism. They have given racial pride to Black youth, and in their dramatic assertion of the right to bear arms in self-defense have electrified the ghetto with a new fighting spirit. They have played an important role in offsetting the degrading effects of ghetto environment—the tendency to become demoralized, to try to "escape" by means of liquor or drugs, and to view *all* of society as the enemy. In other words, the Black Panther Party has struggled to keep Black youth from sinking into the warped state of mind of a totally declassed people. Plank Number Two of the Panther's ten point-program reads: "We want full employment for our people!" This is proof, if proof be needed, that the Black Panthers did not succumb to, let alone glorify, the lumpen condition. They fought against it.

The lumpen condition, as we understand it, is not only a state of material deprivation and oppression. Nor is it merely a state of long-time joblessness. It is also a state of mind affected by a divorce from gainful, productive labor, and by a feeling of hopelessness over this condition. It is a frame of mind that has lost the desire to work, *all* work, and has adopted in its place a scornful, despising attitude to those who do work. It is a deteriorating process in which living by whatever means comes to hand is not only accepted as a matter of necessity, but as a glorified life style. Thus we disagree with Cleaver when he says that the Black Panther Party has been the representative of the lumpens. It has represented those who have been fighting against becoming lumpens, or those who have pulled themselves out of this status and begun to see the world and their role in it from a revolutionary socialist point of view.

It is important to make these distinctions because no one—not even the Black Panther Party, as recent events have shown—is immune from the influences of the environment. Operating in the milieu of the street among young people who are unemployed and many of whom have never worked, subject to the influences and pressures of the lumpen stratum all around them, the Black Panther Party has become infiltrated by lumpen ideology. Cleaver has become its main theoretical exponent. He tends to glorify the lumpen status. In so doing he actually accepts and glorifies the Ronald Reagan caricature of the poor, whether Black, Brown, Red, Yellow or white.

How the Black Panther Party handles this question of class ideology will determine its future. Without a clear class view of the struggle it will find that the lumpen environment in which it operates will have more of an effect on it than it on this environment. This is not to deny the revolutionary potential inherent in the "street people." Nor is it to deny that portions of them can at times be more militant and more desirous of revolutionary change than other strata of the population. Their conditions of life are so volatile that spontaneous eruptions are inevitable. Yet these conditions are also such as to make them an extremely unreliable mass. Marx, in *Class Struggles in France,* written in 1850, referred to the young people of the lumpen stratum as "thoroughly malleable, as capable of the most heroic deeds and the most exalted sacrifices as of the basest banditry and the dirtiest corruption" (p. 50). Thus, whether they are to be molded into revolutionaries depends upon the existence of an ideologically firm Marxist-Leninist vanguard capable of doing the molding.

Yet with the best of molding in the world, the lumpens cannot make or lead the revolution. Only the working class, Black, Brown and white, can be the *main* social agency for revolution. And only leaders who grasp this truth—it is immaterial whether they come from the ranks of the working class or not—can lead such a revolution.

This belief does not flow from any sort of "labor mystique." We do not believe that a worker is more noble, honest, intelligent, or capable than other people. But there is no other class in modern society that can *down* the capitalist class, *keep* it down, and undertake to reconstruct society along collectivist lines. Other strata of the population may be more downtrodden, more oppressed; other social strata may at times have a greater will to revolt, but no other class or stratum has the capacity to paralyze the system at the point of production, where it hurts the most, and establish a new economy based on production for public use instead of private corporate profit. It is the only class with the numbers, the organizational compactness, the technological know-how, the strategic location and potential cohesion and discipline, with which to wield a comparable counterpower to that of the owning class. When harnessed to a conscious goal its power can be greater than that of the ruling class, especially when united with natural allies from other oppressed and discontented sections of the population. The lumpens can demonstrate, riot, even burn things down; they cannot and do not have the power to down the system and to build a new one. Cleaver says that a rejection of the lumpens as the leading revolutionary force arises from "prejudiced analysis made from the narrow perspectives of the working class." But this assertion answers nothing. His viewpoint too can be charged to a prejudiced analysis made from the narrow perspectives of the lumpens. The questions we must ask and answer are: What is the nature of the present society? What is necessary to revolutionize and replace it with a higher social order?

The society in which we live is more than ideological-cultural-psychological. It is more than just an immoral, depraved system of ideas. It is in the first place an economic system. The main classes of any society are those that play the main roles in the process of production and exchange. Under capitalism these are the bourgeoisie and the working class. Capitalist society cannot exist without both of these classes. There can be no capitalists without workers any more than, under this system, there can be wage workers without capitalists. To revolutionize society requires that the system of production and exchange be revolutionized so that the capitalists can be eliminated forever. The only class that can accomplish this, that can reorganize production and distribution on a new foundation, both without and against the capitalists, is the working class. No other class can fulfill this role. And when we speak of the working class we are not narrowly referring to industrial or manual workers alone, but to all in this society who must sell their physical or mental work-ability to an employer in order to live.

Furthermore, only to the extent that the working class does play the leading political role, is there any hope of winning the other fringe classes, including sections of the lumpen stratum, for constructive revolutionary ends. It is the magnet that alone can pull the links of disparate social forces toward a common objective. Without it, the magnetic pull is all in the opposite class direction.

Cleaver is certainly right when he says that to set one's orientation on the working class determines one line of tactics, and to set it on the lumpens, another. To make the dope-pushers, muggers, petty thieves, and those who detest working for a living, the basis for the building of a revolutionary party and revolutionary strategy and tactics, is absurd. It is to try to build a solid, stable movement with the least solid and stable of human elements.

Cleaver argues that it is not in the factories and workshops but in the streets that the revolution will be made. To think that "street people" can make the revolution without the participation of, or against the will of, the working people in the factories and workshops is ridiculous. Cleaver believes that the "street people" are best equipped to be the "true revolutionaries" because the lumpen "has no immediate oppressor except perhaps the Pig Police with which it is confronted daily." But the "Pig Police" is not the oppressor, only the hired tool of the oppressing *class*. He is a *symbol* of the oppressive system, but he is not *the* oppressor. The one-sided stress on "the pig" is only expressive of a one-sided, oversimplified view of our society.

Cleaver writes: "The Lumpen is forced to create its own forms of rebellion that are consistent with its condition in life and with its relationship to the means of production and the institutions of society. That is, to strike out at all the structures around it, including the reactionary Right Wing of the Proletariat when it gets in the way of revolution" (Cleaver, 1970). As Cleaver believes the working class to be the right wing of the proletariat, he is thus envisioning a collision between street people and workers. Such a collision would not only be with white workers, but also with Black, for the Black workers, too, according to Cleaver, are part of the right wing of the proletariat.

Thus Cleaver's strategy begins and ends with the lumpens.

5. Black Workers

WHAT IS incomprehensible about Cleaver's analysis is his failure to note the *main* trend among Black people and what this trend may portend for the future. It is simply not true that the majority of Black people are lumpens. The great majority are workers. A predominantly rural people only a few decades ago, the Black people today are more working class in their composition than any other group of the population.

We have indicated previously that the technological changes of recent years have increased the number of Black unemployed and unemployables. The movement from the land to the cities has also jammed additional millions into the already crowded Northern and Southern ghettos. But this is only one side of the technological effects. The other side is a radical alteration in employment patterns. There has been a shift from employment in the industrial, physical-labor jobs, to those in the professional and white-collar fields. With more and more white youth seeking the softer jobs, and with discrimination operating against Black youth getting them, the latter have been compelled to take over the heavier, dirtier, more dangerous and lower paying industrial and physical-labor jobs.

The net result of this process has produced a new development—the Black workers are now a major force at the point of production. In one industry after another the proportion of Black workers has increased and in some they are a large minority and even close to a majority. Urban and interurban public transit is now operated largely by Black and other minority workers. In the civil services, too, especially the postal service, the percentage of Black workers is exceedingly high. Likewise in the major auto plants in Detroit, the steel mills in the Middle West, the needle trades in New York, the hotels, restaurants and hospitals throughout nation, the number and proportion of nonwhite workers is constantly growing.*

This must be related to another important fact. Poverty in the Black communities does not stem from mass unemployment alone. The President's Commission on Civil Disorders has estimated that the greater source of poverty comes from *under*-employment and from *low wages*. The Report states that "the single most important source of poverty among Negroes" is the "concentration of male employment at the lowest end of the occupational scale."† The Report concentrates on male employment, but it is a well-known fact that the Black women workers, whether in hospitals, textile mills, as household employees, or in the needle trades in New York, are at the very bottom of the wage scale.

To treat these workers as "the Right Wing of the proletariat," is travesty. To ignore their struggle is shortsightedness. To fail to see the latent potential of this Black section of the working class vis-a-vis the economic system, and its strategic position vis-à-vis

---

*In 1960, 13.4 per cent of machine operatives were Black; in 1969, it was 16.9 per cent. In 1960, 33.9 per cent of the Black labor force were machine operatives and nonfarm laborers as compared to 22 per cent of the white labor force. In 1969, 34.4 per cent of Blacks were so employed and only 21.8 per cent of whites. In 1960, 33.3 per cent of farm labor was Black; in 1969 the proportion was 22.7 per cent. Thus the industrial working class composition of the Black population has been increasing steadily (From statistics of the U.S. Department of Labor and the U.S. Department of Commerce).

†"If every one of these persons [nonwhite unemployed] had been employed and had received the median amount earned by nonwhite males in 1966 ($3,864), this would have added a total of $2.7 billion to nonwhite income as a whole. . . . But if nonwhite unemployment remained at 7.3 per cent, and nonwhite men were upgraded so that they had the same occupational distribution and incomes as all men in the labor force considered together, this would have produced about $4.8 billion in additional income" (Report of the *President's Commission on National Disorders*, p. 255).

the white workers, is to see things from the narrow perspectives of the lumpen stratum. To separate oneself from the problems and struggles of these workers—and to do this in the holy name of revolution—is blindness indeed.

The nationwide wildcat strike of postal workers in the spring of 1970 was largely spearheaded by Black workers. In the auto and steel industries the Black workers are forming their own caucuses and organizations and are conducting a struggle against racism on the job and in the union. The Black Caucus movement is spreading from one industry to another. Talk about Black Power! Here is where it's at. And here too is where an alliance between Black and white workers will in time be forged around the issues of common concern.

It is true that there is more pent-up resentment and despair among the unemployable. Certainly their conditions and needs should be an issue of urgent concern and action, and not on their part alone. But this requires not merely shouting for *revolution now*, but also organizing the fight for *jobs now*. Thus the problems of one group need not be ignored for the problems of the other. But from the viewpoint of perspective—revolutionary perspective!—the task of bringing consciousness to the working class and giving leadership to the workers' struggles is the most important of all tasks. True, it will be more difficult and frustrating for a period of time, but he who calls himself a revolutionist should not shirk from the more difficult, especially if it is the most decisive, task.

6. In the Good Old Days of Karl Marx

THE WORKING class of our time, declares Cleaver, "has become a new industrial elite." But certainly he cannot be speaking of the millions of Black workers who do the hardest work and receive the lowest pay. Are these too part of the "elite?" Yet he never considers them as part of his answer, only as part of the problem.

The flames of revolution "once raged like an inferno in the heart of the Working Class," continues Cleaver, but today it shows "little resemblance to the Working Class in Marx's day."

The working class today, he insists, "is a parasite upon the heritage of mankind" (Cleaver, 1970). Strangely, Cleaver says little about the real parasites of our society, the corporate monopolies that own and run the country. Nor does he recognize the existence of any sort of class struggle, not even a tiny wee-bit of one. According to his way of thinking the workers are all fat-cats that have it made.

There is truth, of course, to the observation that the working class today is not what it was in Marx's time. It is the same *class*, but its condition of life and its class outlook have undergone change. But this generalization, like all such, hides an oversimplification. The working class in Marx's day did not all exude revolutionary fire and brimstone. It too had more than its share of illusions, and the labor movement more than its share of corruption, opportunism and venality. Dozens of letters and articles of Marx and Engels covering a period of forty-odd years detail their concern with the situation in the English working-class movement. In 1890, Engels referred to the 40 years' "long winter sleep" of the British working class. Earlier, he had scornfully accused the English workers of "becoming more and more bourgeois."*

---

*In 1858, Marx wrote about "the inertia which at present pervades the working class in England." In that same year, Engels noted that "The English proletariat is becoming more and more bourgeois." In 1863, Marx was not sure how soon the English workers "will free themselves from their apparent bourgeois infection." In 1868, Engels deplored that, "Everywhere the proletariat are the tag, rag and bobtail of the official parties." After the death of one of the better labor leaders in 1869, Engels feared that the workers "will become completely disintegrated again and fall right into the net of the bourgeoisie." Thirteen years later, in 1882, he wrote: "You ask me what the English workers think about colonial policy. Well, exactly the same as they think about politics in general: the same as what the bourgeois think. There is no workers' party here, there are only Conservatives and Liberal-Radicals, and the workers gaily share the feast of England's monopoly of the world market and the colonies." In 1889, he once more stressed that "The most replusive thing here is the bourgeois 'respectability' that has grown deep in the bones of the workers." Yet with the rise of the "new unionism" of the unskilled workers he noted that "these unskilled are very different chaps from the fossilized brothers of the old craft unions." (*Selected Correspondence*, for numerous references to labor opportunism in England; pp. 33-36, 100-02, 115-16, 146-48, 254, 355-58, 399, 419-22, 461-62, 488, 505-06.)

While acquainted most intimately with the English working-class movement, Marx and Engels had occasion to strike out at ignorance, backwardness, opportunism and corruption in the working-class movements of other countries as well. Sharply criticizing the draft of the Erfurt Program adopted by the German Social-Democratic Party in 1891, Engels warned that "this struggling and striving for the success of the moment without consideration for the later consequences, this sacrifice of the future of the movement for its present may be 'honestly' meant, but it is and remains opportunism and 'honest' opportunism is perhaps the most dangerous of all" (*Selected Correspondence*, p. 486).

Most interesting in many respects is the letter which Marx wrote to his friend Kugelman, on October 9, 1866, about the Parisian workers and the role they had played at the first congress of the International Working Men's Association (the First International). Marx characterized their behavior as "Ignorant, vain, presumptuous, chattering, dogmatic, arrogant, they were at the point of spoiling everything." As workers in the luxury trades, Marx explained, they "are closely attached, without knowing it, to the old muck" (p. 194).

It is worth remembering this incident for what happened less than six years later. The Paris workers rose in their might and set up the first workers' state, the Paris Commune. And Marx, who had spoken so harshly of them in 1866, this time used words of deep emotion and immortal praise. He said that workingmen's Paris would never be forgotten, for it had "stormed the heavens." We cite these facts only to refute a rather oversimplified view of the working class of Marx's day. But neither do we want to oversimplify the working class of our day. The situation has changed vastly, especially in the United States. Were it otherwise there would not be the frantic search for another social agency to do what only the working class can do.

CHAPTER VIII

HOW STRONG IS THE TIGER?

1. The New Illusions

THOSE WHO believe as do Marcuse and Cleaver that the working class has lost the potential to be the revolutionary class, apparently believe that modern capitalism has achieved perpetual economic motion—it has ironed out the kinks in the economic system. This, at bottom, explains much of the false pessimism of Marcuse and the false optimism of Cleaver.* Despite considerable talk about American imperialism being a "paper tiger," there is a great exaggeration of the tiger's strength and prowess. It is neither all-paper nor all-powerful. It is a wounded beast, even more dangerous because infuriated. But it is wounded.

As we have seen, Marcuse explicitly believes that modern technological capitalism can now meet the basic needs of all and thereby contain effective protest and revolt. Cleaver says it implicitly. He believes that this has already happened for the workers and that the only exceptions are the lumpens. But if the system is capable of meeting the needs of *all*, why not also the lumpens? If it is threatened by imminent revolution on the part of the lumpens, as Cleaver believes, would it not bribe this stratum also? Or are we to believe that lumpens are less susceptible to being bribed than are workers?

If it is true that the system can now meet the needs of all, or that this is the trend, then Marcuse is right: the system will use such ability to contain the movement for qualitative change. But

*"The swiftly developing revolution in America is like the gathering of a mighty storm, and nothing can stop that storm from finally bursting, inside America, washing away the pigs of the power structure and all their foul, oppressive works. And the children of the pigs and the oppressed people will dance and spit upon the common graves of these pigs" (Cleaver, 1970).

we challenge the assumption that it can and that this is the direction in which things are moving.

The period of 1872 to 1914, broadly speaking, was one of relative "peaceful" development for Western capitalism. The "peace" was based on a system of brutal colonial enslavement, but it was, nonetheless, a period of relative calm in which rapid technological change was ushering in an era of monopoly domination. It was in this epoch of capitalist expansion, of high profits and high wages, that Edward Bernstein, a German socialist and one-time collaborator of Marx and Engels, developed a revisionist departure from Marxism. He believed that capitalism was now solving its basic contradictions, especially the class contradiction, and that the path ahead would be one of gradual peaceful development and reform until capitalism had been metamorphosed into socialism. Lenin fought Bernsteinism. Reviewing a book on the subject in 1899, he agreed with its author, Karl Kautsky, that "Bernstein ascribes to purely temporary conditions of a given historical situation the dignity of a general law" ("A Review of Kautsky's Book," p. 203).

This observation of Lenin is important to remember. The period we have been living through has by no means been peaceful. It has been a stormy one, of wars and revolutions. Yet there are features of the post-World War II period that have led to new false assumptions about the stability of the system and its ability to contain its internal contradictions.

In many ways it has been a unique period. Pre-World War II capitalism was characterized by periodic cyclical economic crises. The one that began in October 1929, was of longer duration, more acute, and more worldwide in scope than any economic crisis in the history of capitalism. But since World War II capitalism has avoided the outbreak of another devastating economic crisis. There have been a number of recessions, but these were mild compared with the wild plunges of the past.

This is something new. Never before in the history of capitalism has a deep economic crisis been avoided for so long a period of time, a full quarter of a century. It is this which provides the soil from which the new illusions have sprung. It is the main source of illusions within the working class as it is among intellectuals who have "given up" on the working class in the very name of revolution. These latter assume that by flattening the economic cycle capitalism has eliminated deep economic crises for all times and with them the acute class struggle in society. Thus, *a la* Bernstein, they too "ascribe to purely temporary conditions of a given historical situation the dignity of a general law." A number of factors have contributed to the lengthy postwar boom and relative economic stability. The war was followed by a pent-up worldwide demand for goods and services and a need to retool obsolescent plants and equipment. The rapid growth of world population and the emergence of scores of newly formed States at various levels of economic development have also spurred the expansion of world markets. There has been likewise a steady large-scale migration of U.S. capital abroad in the form of investments in foreign enterprises on a scale dwarfing anything in the past.*

An extremely great impact has been provided by the revolution in science and technology in the advanced countries which some have called "a third industrial revolution." This has absorbed immense investment funds in electronics and cybernetics; in transportation and communication; and in the atomic energy, space, chemical, plastics and related industries. Whole new branches of industry have sprung to life and no industry has been left untouched by the giant hand of scientific and technical advance.

Another major factor has been the balloon-like expansion of credit, both public and private. The public debt has increased from $140 billion in 1945 to $566 billion in 1960, to $1,247 billion in 1969. Private corporate debt has grown from $142 billion in 1950 to $692 billion in 1969. Mortgages—mainly home mortgages—have jumped from $45 billion in 1950 to $262 billion in 1968. Consumer credit has leaped from $21.5 billion in 1950 to $113 billion in 1968 (*Statistical Abstract,* 1970, pp. 394, 437).

---

*U.S. assets and investments abroad reached $54 billion in 1950 and were estimated at $146 billion in 1968. Private foreign investments were $19 billion in 1950 and $102 billion in 1968 (*Statistical Abstract,* 1970, p. 765).

2. Role of Government Spending

YET ALL these combined, as important as they are, would not have been sufficient to modify the gyrations of the economic cycle. One more thing was needed: large scale, permanent, government intervention in the economy as the main controlling lever of economic policy. Without this new role of the government many of the previously mentioned factors could not have played the role they did. Foreign investment, for example, has been partly financed and underwritten by the government. Billions of dollars of public funds have been spent annually to dump American goods abroad in the name of so-called "aid," but in reality as a means of greasing the chute for U.S. corporations. Additional billions have been lavishly handed out to buy, bribe, and arm so-called "friendly" governments and to make them safe for American corporate investments. Government funds, too, have largely financed the research projects so needed if science and technology were to race ahead at full speed. As for the atomic energy and space programs, these have been financed entirely out of the public till.

But the largest impact of government intervention has been in the form of huge military expenditures.* These have served a dual purpose—to build up military hardware with which to lay claim to world supremacy and with which to defend U.S. corporate interests abroad† and secondly as the most important anti-depression remedy.

Government expenditures for military purposes have certain advantages for the ruling class. In the first place, military production is exceedingly profitable. It has a guaranteed market and through corporate-Pentagon interlocking relations prices can be set just about at will. Because arms production creates no

*Federal budget outlays for national defense were $13 billion in 1950, $46 billion in 1960, and $81 billion in 1969.
†"I believe the United States can't be a world power—which we are—with half world interests. We are an Asian power, a Pacific power. It takes a growing up on the part of liberal intellectuals—the liberal and articulate spokesmen—to see our relationship to the Asian area and the fact that we are and have to be involved (Hubert Humphrey, "Interview," *Christian Science Monitor*, August 16, 1966).

useful goods or services it does not compete with marketable commodities and therefore cannot glut the market. It is a production of pure waste. But for this production of waste great quantities of raw materials and human labor are required. Thus armament production is inflationary in its effect, for immense resources are taken out of the economy and no new values are put back in their stead.

One of the first proposals for the setting up of a "permanent war economy" in the United States came in the midst of World War II. The war had finally pulled the United States out of ten long years of depression. Even more than previous wars, this one had been a great boon to U.S. capitalism and had opened for it new vistas of world power. Sensing all this, Charles E. Wilson of General Electric delivered a speech in January 1944 to the Army Ordnance Association. He urged an alliance of the military, the executive branch of the government, and the large corporations. He proposed that every large corporation have a colonel in the reserves on its roster for liason with the military. Industry's role was to cooperate in the execution of the program, but to do so required that it not be hampered "by political witch hunts," or be "tagged with a 'merchants of death' label" (Dibble, 1967).

It is a commentary on the nature of our society that the wholesale production of means of destruction is seen as a major answer to preventing deep-going economic crises. Yet there are some who have read into the government's more active intervention in economic life a sign of the basic health of the system—an example of its flexibility, its capacity for self-correction, its ability to apply the brakes or push down the accelerator on the economic mechanism. It is the opposite, of course. It is a sign of how chronic and desperate is the system's plight, for it is no longer capable of operating in either a normal or rational fashion.

The paramount contradiction of capitalist society is between production which assumes an ever more social (collective) character and accumulation which still remains private (corporate). This basic antagonism can be resolved in only one way—by society itself taking possession of the means of production. But the economic measures of state monopoly capitalism are not meant to resolve this conflict. They are meant to prolong the system of private accumulation while augmenting the share grabbed by the huge monopoly corporations.

Yet by assuming public responsibility for keeping the economy out of the ditch, the State has made an oblique admission. It has said, in effect, that the answer to the anarchy of capitalist production lies only in the direction of greater social controls. This acknowledgement is exceedingly important and has now entered into the public consciousness. Thus far it has fed the illusion that capitalist government intervention *is* that social control. But what will happen when this proves to be the fantasy it is?

3. New Tensions in Place of Old

WATERS THAT are dammed up cannot be held back indefinitely. Blocked in one direction they pour forth in others. This is now happening. The measures adopted to prevent an economic debacle have already precipitated a number of social crises without removing the menace of an economic crash. This latter fact can be seen by projecting ahead the curve of one of the factors that have held back depression. We have indicated previously that credit, including consumer credit (installment buying), has been expanding like a balloon. In dollar and cents terms this has meant the following: in 1946, immediately following the big war, only 6 cents out of every consumer dollar went to pay debts; by 1960, this had skyrocketed to 18 cents out of every dollar; and in 1969, it had claimed 23 cents out of every dollar. In other words, nearly one-fourth of current income goes to pay for past purchases! How long can this continue and how much higher can it go? It does not take much imagination to figure out what can happen if unemployment continues to increase, and if prices and the cost of living continue to mount.

We are now witnessing a steady erosion of every one of the factors that has held back a major depression. These are closely intertwined and what happens to one immediately affects the rest. The psychology of inflation leads to wholesale speculation—to the reckless inflation of paper values in the expectation that the continuation of the boom will make the gamble pay off. The conglomerate mania of recent years is a case in point. As long as the boom psychology lasted everything went. People fell for the hogwash that greater efficiency and higher profit yields can be attained by merging pickle and ice cream companies with Broadway productions and steel corporations. For a while it seemed to work. As nothing succeeds like success, and as the success of the conglomerates seemed assured, the rush to buy stocks in them only made their "success" a certainty, at least while the bubble lasted. For a few of them the day of reckoning has already come as one after another undergoes "reorganizations," as brokerage firms teeter on the brink, and as mighty corporations like Chrysler, Lockheed and Penn-Central beg the government to bail them out.* It is only a beginning.

Assuming the government still has the reserves and the manipulative means—with public funds—to forestall an old fashioned economic depression, at what costs and with what consequences?

The effects of technological change and the growth in unemployment, the diversion of public funds from social needs to militarism and warfare, the constant rise in prices and taxes as part of a general inflation, have already taken their toll. A series of deep-going social crises, affecting and arousing ever larger numbers of people, has produced a questioning of the system unparalleled in our country's history. First, there is the intense crisis of our ghettos and our poor which merges, but is not identical, with a profound crisis in race relations. Then there is a crisis of our central cities which merges with a governmental crisis in federal-state-local relations. There is a breakdown in delivery of basic social services—health, housing, education, transportation, air and water pollution, conservation, and so forth. And on top of these there is a permanent crisis in foreign relations with a series of war crises of which Indochina is but the latest. It also has begotten the monstrous growth of the Pentagon

*This is "socialism for the rich." At a time when the ruling class attacks giving welfare for the poor, it has no compunctions whatever to ask for increased welfare for its own class brothers "in trouble."

and the constant danger of a world nuclear war and an American type of military-fascist rule.

The drain of wealth for destructive instead of constructive ends has so depleted the country that Seymour Melman has called it, with good reason, "our depleted society." This is a far more accurate description of what is taking place than that which insists on referring to the United States as the "post-industrial society" or the "overdeveloped society." The dialectics of it is that an overdevelopment of one kind has led to an underdevelopment of another.

Melman puts it this way: "Since 1945, the United States spent $1,100 billion for military purposes, of which the war in Vietnam accounts for about $150 billion. *$1,100 billion exceeds the value of all business and residential structures in the United States*" (emphasis added). Economists, he believes, have misled themselves and the nation by measuring economic growth by the rise of the GNP (Gross National Product). But

the rise of G.N.P. from $503 billion in 1960 to $932 billion in 1969 does not distinguish between growth that is economically productive and the growth that is parasitic. Productive growth includes goods and services that form part of the level of living, or that can be used for further production. By this economic-functional criterion, apart from other yardsticks, goods and services that are *not* part of the level of living or *cannot* be used for further production are economically parasitic.

Having given priority in public budgets and technical talent to $1,100 billion of parasitic growth, this nation is now reaping a whirlwind of economic and human depletion (Seymour Melman, "Pax-Americana II: Cost of Militarism", *New York Times*, November 3, 1970).

Hardly a city is not in deep financial trouble and, under present conditions, has anywhere else to go but to greater trouble. The residential communities where the working class poor live, particularly the Black, Chicano and Puerto Rican poor, are literally rotting, while only a short distance away, in the business districts, newer and taller skyscrapers pierce the smog. It is similar to what happened during the decay of the Roman Empire—the rise of majestic marble palaces and great architectural triumphs on one side, while deterioration and squalor spread on the other side.

There is more to the urban crisis than the wasteful expenditures of tax money for militarism and war, but the latter is a major contributing element to this crisis. "The Federal government now collects two-thirds of total revenues, while the municipal share has fallen from 52 per cent in 1932 to less than 7 per cent today" (*New Republic*, October 7, 1967). In 1968, local governments collected $48 billion in taxes, had expenditures of $72 billion, and outstanding debts of $85 billion. But in 1950, local government debts totalled only $19 billion (*Statistical Abstract*, 1970, p. 402). The designation "local governments" also includes counties, villages and towns, as well as the urban suburbs. All of these are in financial distress, although the central cities are in the most desperate condition of all. Every local government suffers to one degree or another from the lion's share of the tax revenue being devoured by the Federal government, from the failure to place the tax burden on the rich, and from spending for parasitic ends.

These facts suffice to show the consequences of anti-social policies. But something more is now happening. Inflation, originally looked upon as an antidote to depression, is now a factor inducing a creeping recession that may well turn into a major depression. There is good reason for this. War-kindled inflation is self-perpetuating. At first it has a stimulating effect on the economy, flushing its cheeks and giving it an appearance of ruddy good health. After a while, however, as with all stimulants, it turns into a depressant. When this takes place it becomes necessary to try to put inflation under control. If this is not done, a financial crisis could act as the kick-off to an old-fashioned type depression.

Inflation has now reached a point at which any further increase in the cost of living will further inflame the present areas of acute social tension, drawing the vast majority of the people into the vortex of class and social conflict. It is bound to produce strike wave after strike wave. Where these lead to substantial wage increases they only become the pretexts for further hikes in prices. Further inflation will also exacerbate the problem of the federal budget, forcing drastic cuts and/or a new rise in deficit spending. It will materially add to the cost of the war and thereby increase the mass pressure against the war. The ability of state and local governments to make ends meet will become more strained, creating more breakdowns in social services, more resentment among government employees, and more government borrowing from the banks. Continued inflation will likewise tend to price U.S. goods out of foreign markets and turn more American buyers to foreign-made products. And all this would make the balance of payments problem even more acute, weaken the dollar as world currency, and lower the prestige of U.S. imperialism abroad.*

Runaway inflation could be stemmed. There is a simple way of doing this—end the war in Vietnam and with it the swollen military expenditures. But this is just about the last thing being contemplated. It would weaken the U.S. empire at a time when the economy seeks expanding markets, full control over foreign sources of raw materials, and new investment opportunities abroad.

Nixon would like to tighten up the military operation to make it more efficient, but under no circumstances does he want it weakened. He would like to cut losses in Indochina, reduce the number of Americans fighting there, shift more of the fighting burden to the Vietnamese mercenaries, but has no intention of completely pulling out. In time, political-military events in Indochina and the pressure of the American people at home will compel this. But even then there will be no assurance of a major reduction in military expenditures. Already now, in the preparation for such an eventuality, plans are being laid to make sure that a pull-out in Vietnam does not lead anyone to conclude that U.S. global military power has waned.

Hanson Baldwin, the military expert of the *New York Times* and a man with an inside track to the Pentagon, discussed this as far back as 1968. He wrote:

---

*"European governments have been serving notice on the United States that they will not go on accepting extra billions of paper dollars to cover huge United States balance-of-payments deficits, of which inflation is a basic cause. The Europeans also have pressed the United States to adopt an incomes policy" (Leonard Silk, *New York Times*, November 15, 1970).

No matter how the war in Vietnam ends—the continent of Asia and its bordering islands and surrounding seas and oceans will remain for decades the stage of political, economic or military conflict. Asia and the Western Pacific have become a new global power center which, in time, will transcend Europe in importance, and the future—not alone of the United States, but of the world—will to an increasing degree depend upon what happens in Asia.

We live in "time of troubles" and we cannot make them go away by pulling the covers over our heads . . . . We are in the Western Pacific and Asia to stay.

How is the military crisis in Asia to be met? By military "technological escalation" to meet the "unfavorable manpower balance in Asia," he answered. And he warned that technological escalation will cost money, lots of money. "No such policy can be accomplished on the cheap; it will cost the taxpayer money, for this is the price of power" (Baldwin, "After Vietnam—What Military Strategy in the Far East").

C. L. Sulzberger of the *New York Times* makes an even more sinister forecast. In an article "Solving the Ugly Dilemma," he says that the great lesson of Vietnam is that the United States can no longer maintain its many commitments abroad and its foreign policy aims with the kind of military establishment, strategy or network of alliances now employed. He quotes defense department experts who believe that this country "will either have to increase qualitatively our ability to respond to local threats, or in the future we will have to see a substantial reduction in our commitments and influence over the course of events." By "local threats" is meant *any* threat to the status quo in any part of the capitalist-dominated world. There is no threat to the territorial security of the United States.

Sulzberger is gung-ho for a qualitative increase in the U.S. military ability to meet such "threats." As total nuclear war "cannot be contemplated except as the ultimate deterrent" (whatever that means), Sulzberger believes that something in between "conventional warfare" and total nuclear disaster has to be found. "The answer may well lie in the field of truly tactical atomic weapons." Such research, he indicates, is under way today to find " 'fusion-enhanced radiation' or 'neutron' warheads

with relatively lower blast and heat collateral effects." He
concludes: "There seems to be no middle road between supine-
ness and suicide" (C. L. Sulzberger, *New York Times,* November
15, 1970).

And so, frustrated by military failures in Indochina, and aware
of the revolutionary process at work all over the imperialist
dominated world, U.S. imperialism can no longer limit itself to
"conventional weapons" such as napalm, chemical warfare,
billions of tons of bombs dropped on civilian populations, and
Mylai massacres. It now aims for even more monstrous genocidal weapons.

Hence it can be seen that the dilemma and crisis of U.S.
imperialism are deeper and more profound in some respects than
for other, less powerful, imperialist-capitalist States. France
could back out of Indochina and Algeria quite gracefully, after
being compelled to do so by the people of these two areas and
after surmounting a governmental crisis in France itself. Britain,
too, was capable of bowing out as the world's greatest colonial
empire. But U.S. imperialism is determined to succeed where the
others failed. It is determined to take over the remnants of the old
colonial empires and to hold back the tides of revolution by
whatever means are necessary.

4. The Outlook Ahead

WHILE IT will fail in this attempt as it has failed up to now, the
outlook for the period ahead is of unremitting struggle. Unable to
stop inflation and increase military expenditures at one and the
same time, the Nixon Administration is compelled to try to check
inflation by the only way open to it: increasingly placing the cost
of empire-building on the backs of the people. As Hanson
Baldwin stressed, "it will cost the taxpayer money, for this is the
price of power."

It is the recognition of this truth by the dominant monopolist
sections of the ruling class that explains the sharp "turn to the
Right" of the Nixon Administration. It explains the get-tough-
with-students policy, the calculated use of armed violence while

charging the Left with violence, and the murder of many Black, Chicano and Puerto Rican militant leaders. It also explains the attempts to whip up a new McCarthyite hysteria, to stir up the embers of the Cold War, and the cynical and monstrous frame-ups of Angela Davis, Bobby Seale, Ericka Huggins, the Berrigan brothers, and many others.

When the ruling class decides to make concessions to popular pressure it adopts a so-called "soft" policy. This does not exclude getting tough when necessary, but the main direction of policy is "soft." When the ruling class is determined not to grant major concessions, when such concessions stand in the way of its most important interests as it sees them, it turns to a so-called "hard" policy. This, too, does not exclude concessions when necessary, but these do not characterize the main line of policy. Demagogy is still used—is always used!—but it is of a somewhat different kind. It no longer makes the same grandiose promises about a war on poverty, decent housing for all, full employment, and so forth. Such demagogy can be dangerous. People may believe it and then go on to demand it.

The policy of getting tough with the ghetto is necessary because the ruling class does not intend to give jobs, decent housing, or to meet the other needs of the people. Getting tough with the students is also called for if the intention is to remain in Indochina, to escalate military expenditures, and to continue to outrage the moral sensibilities of young people.

Getting tough cannot stop with the ghetto and the campus. The refusal to reverse priorities and meet domestic needs must inevitably deepen the many areas of social crises and increase mass resentment and opposition. Continued inflation will be felt most of all by the people on welfare, social security and limited fixed incomes, but all working people and lower income groups will feel its effects. Thus the workers' pressure for higher take-home pay is bound to increase. So also will the government's attempts to "hold the line" on wages. A collision is therefore inevitable. But an attack on labor cannot be carried out in the same way as an attack upon students or the ghetto. Power respects power; organization respects organization. The ruling class cannot ignore the latent power inherent in organized labor. Thus stealth and deception are called for. Blows aimed at workers' living standards must be made to appear, to some of them at least, as in their own best interests. And pretensions of friendship for labor must abound while top labor brass gets wined, dined and flattered and at the same time warned not to rock the boat.

If wages are to be "kept in line," a so-called "incomes policy" must be imposed sooner or later. In words at least this will aim to curb both higher prices and higher wages. In effect, however, its real purpose will be to freeze wages while enabling increased productivity and a "controlled" inflation to eat away at workers' real buying power. Nothing will be done to really curb exhorbitant corporate profits.

Liberal economists and congressmen have been calling for wage-price controls. It is only a matter of time before the Administration bows before their request. And this is surely to be followed by efforts aimed at further restricting the right to use the strike weapon.

This certainly is not the scenario for domestic peace and tranquility. Sharp class and social struggles are inevitable. And let us ask: What can the ruling class accomplish by a policy of lowering the standard of living and imposing the burden of armaments on the people? Only ever growing unemployment and the very economic disaster it so anxiously seeks to avert. Or, a major war crisis that will shake the very foundations of American society.

Yes, the tiger is still powerful and extremely dangerous, but also mighty sick. A great deal depends, however, on how it is fought. That is the subject of our next chapter.

CHAPTER IX

AN APPROACH TO STRATEGY

WITHOUT A common approach to strategy it is impossible to build a common Movement. A common approach to strategy is needed to help pull together the present disparate, amorphous, confused and divided Movement into a serious, on-going and growing force for revolutionary change. This is why the ideological battle for a common approach to strategy is so important at this time.

Our stress is on the world "approach." It is impossible to achieve unity on all aspects of strategy, yet we must know the main direction we want to go and how to begin to get there. Without this, even the accelerated motion of periodic upheavals leads nowhere. As in Alice in Wonderland it takes all the running we can do to stay in the same place. But in politics—and every challenge to power is politics—there is no such thing as staying in the same place. Either one moves forward or gets shoved backward.

There is another reason for stress on the word "approach." None of us has as yet found the path to a mass revolutionary movement in this country, and all of us at times have made serious blunders in analysis, estimate and judgment. The phrase "none of us" definitely includes this writer, who is painfully aware of his own share of such errors. We wish, therefore, to avoid any appearance of possessing the authoritative last word. There is no last word. It is always in the process of being written.

No one has, nor can claim to have, the map which charts the twists and turns of the revolutionary path ahead. The struggle helps carve its own path. Every battle won, lost, or drawn, changes the terrain of struggle somewhat, alters the stakes involved, compels the contending forces to re-evaluate their positions, to modify or abandon their tactics, and to choose the path to new battles. This may be the broad highway of massive offensive, or the more tortured, twisted path of partial advance or temporary retreat.

During most of the decade of the Sixties the so-called "New Left" blamed the so-called "Old Left" for the debacle of the Fifties and for the failure to "make" the revolution. The "New Left" was convinced that it had the answer to what was wrong and that it was going to succeed where the older generation had failed. But now that we are in the Seventies, the depth of the crisis in which the new radicalism finds itself can no longer be hidden nor ignored. It is a ship tossed by angry seas, without compass to find its bearings or rudder to steer its course. The time has come therefore for all of us to take stock of where we are and where we must go, without the cocksureness or arrogance of someone trying to prove that he or she, or his or her organization has always been right in the past and is necessarily totally right on all questions today.

1. From Organizing to Rhetoric

IN AN article evaluating the Movement, where it is and where it must go, Staughton Lynd comes to the conclusion that the main weakness of the new radicalism has been its failure to organize large masses of people, particularly ordinary people. These, he indicates, are people concerned with problems such as "jobs, children, cars, homes, taxes, and installment payments." Instead of organizing, he believes, the Movement has drifted toward rhetoric (Lynd, "A Program for Post-Campus Radicals").

Lynd is certainly right. Yet we would disagree with him when he seems to think that this failure is unrelated to the question of theory. Answering those who say that the Movement's lack of theory is its main weakness, Lynd replies, "My own criticism (and self-criticism) is almost precisely the reverse".

There can be no doubt that objective conditions played their part in this failure to organize. But the trouble is that the "New Left" made a theory out of its difficulties. This now stands in the way of utilizing the new opportunities that have opened up. It will be impossible to change the situation if the Movement does not see the people as the makers of history, or if it looks down on the problems of ordinary working people and sees them as backward slobs, as part of the Establishment.

While we refer here mainly to the outlook of the white young radicals, the same holds also for some of the revolutionists working among the Black, Chicano and Puerto Rican people. There the possibilities of mass organizing are self-evident, yet the emphasis has been more on the *macho* individual, on his liberating prowess, than on the great mass of the people. The crisis that the Black Panthers find themselves in is a consequence of this same elitist, narrow approach.

Wilfred Burchett, in one of his magnificent books on Vietnam, relates how the Vietnamese sent young Communists to live with the Montagnard mountain people to win them for revolution. They worked and lived amongst them for 25 years, contending with customs that to them seemed strange and even repulsive.

We do not have to wait 25 years to win the people for revolutionary change, nor is it necessary that we live among a strange, foreign people. More than 80 percent of the gainfully employed in this country are working people, either wage or salaried employees. What are missing is the consciousness of this 80 per cent that it is the nation and the will to constitute itself as the nation. But if this consciousness is to be brought to the people there must first be confidence in them.

Soon after the massive invasion of Cambodia, three U.S. war correspondents were captured by Cambodian guerrillas and for more than three weeks taken into the liberated interior. After being released they wrote a series of syndicated articles relating their experiences. All of them were tremendously impressed with the kinship between the guerrillas and the local populace. Richard Dunham, chief Washington correspondent of the St. Louis *Post-Dispatch*, was particularly impressed with their conduct. He wrote: "We noticed that when our guards passed a pagoda they unobtrusively removed their hats. It was a gesture of respect for local religious beliefs—all the more marked, because as we learned later, they were atheists" (*New York Times*, June 24, 1970).

Obviously such conduct could arise only from a deep respect for the people and their customs and the recognition that a revolutionist can only "make" the revolution in the sense of helping the people make it, never as a substitute for the people.

Unless this Marxist theory of revolution is fought for and won in the Movement, as against the petty-bourgeois individualist, anarchist view, there can be neither mass organizing nor a mass movement.

Belief that the people can and will make the revolution requires more than a declaration of faith. It demands a style of work that makes this clear in every word and deed. Without trying to understand what makes the people what they are—why they think and act as they do—it is impossible to have either respect, love or confidence in them.

There are no people that are all good or all bad. No such nation exists nor can exist. Each is a product of history. Each, therefore, is the child of two traditions and two influences—that of degrading, corrupting, oppressing class society, and that of ennobling, heroic, revolutionary and progressive struggle against oppression and exploitation and for freedom. And each of these traditions is in constant struggle with the other.

Because the ruling class needs constantly to bolster the legitimacy of its rule in the eyes of the people, it seeks to distort its past to serve its present. Thus the struggle over tradition is related to the struggle for power itself. The emphasis of young radicals on the negative and reactionary side of American tradition is understandable. It is an effort to counteract the brazen hypocrisy and lies with which the ruling class has concealed its own historic role. Its racist oppression of minority peoples, the pilfering of this nation and the plundering of foreign nations, should all be dealt with and exposed. But the ruling class also distorts the history and struggles of the people; it seeks to bury the revolutionary and progressive side of our traditions—the tradition of Black people, the working people, the various ethnic groups, and so forth. It wishes to hide from the people the fact that every gain they have made was because of their own struggle and not because it was "given" them. And it is important that the people know about the progressive side of their tradition so that they can reject the caricature of themselves handed to them by their exploiters.

To adopt a nihilist position toward one's own people and past is to become a stranger in one's own land. It is to surrender the fight to win the people. It is to mistake those whose minds are poisoned by ideological pollution with the class source of that pollution. If everything in the past of our people has been bad, by what strange logic is one to assume that any good can come from it now or in the future? Such a nihilist position leads only to elitism.

Staughton Lynd does not make this mistake. Yet the point we wish to emphasize again is that these wrong conceptions, whether unconscious or full-blown theories, have a great deal to do with why there has been so little mass organizing.

2. A Lesson From the Thirties

LYND BELIEVES that one of the main reasons why the new radicalism turned from mass organizing to mass rhetoric is that it failed to come to terms with the lessons and experiences of the "Old Left."

I think, [he wrote] we can learn from the older radicals whom we so readily write off but who, nevertheless, organized five million workers into industrial unions and led 500,000 workers in sit-down strikes in 1936-37. The organizers of the 1930s may have something to teach us in just those areas where our own work has been weakest: the building of mass organizations, the bidding for real power.

Lynd's proposed scenario for the 1970s is: "a synthesis of what was best in the political work of the 1960s with what was best in the political work of the 1930s".

Good! This makes sense. Nor should we ignore the 1940s and 1950s. Each decade has something to offer in the form of both positive and negative lessons. Having paid his respects to the generation of the thirties for its mass organizing job, Lynd proceeds to criticize it for what he considers to be its main failings. "The New Left," he believes, "created movement without organization; the Old Left, organization without movement." If there is any doubt as to what he means by this, he spells it out: "The organizers of the 1930s tended to be opportunistic, 'economist.' We of the 1960s have tended to be utopian and adventurist." ("A Program for Post-Campus Radicals.")

It is true that many mistakes were made in the Thirties. These should be analyzed concretely, in the context of the reality in which they took place. To say that there was organization without movement is an oversimplification. It is not possible to have great mass organizations that do not come out of great mass movements. Certainly Lynd cannot mean that only organizations that take a revolutionary stance are to be considered "movement" and all others are to be condemned as "opportunistic."

The organizations of the Thirties were definitely of a mass character. These were not only industrial unions but peoples' organizations of various types—of the unemployed, youth, students, farmers, women, foreign born, small home owners; regional federations in the South and in a number of states; great united front movements for unemployment insurance, Negro rights, for the defense of the Scottsboro Boys, the freedom of Mooney and Billing, for aid to Republican Spain, and against war and fascism. These arose from struggle and served to further the struggle.

To the extent that these were truly of a mass character they were not "created" as a sculptor manipulates pliable clay. Their form and content were determined by events, by vital issues affecting the lives of the people. Where there were sectarian efforts to impose pre-conceived forms on organizations, or more radical and revolutionary programs than they were ready for, the results were invariably disastrous. Only where the Communists learned to abandon a narrow, sectarian approach were they successful in mass organizing.

It is extremely important that this be understood. One of the main reasons there has not been the mass organizing Lynd urges is the fear of building organizations and movements with an inner dialectic and dynamic all of their own and in which there is no guarantee in advance—how can there be?—as to which ideological trend will prevail in the end. It is this fear that often paralyzes the radical movement. It wants a written, signed and sworn assurance that every mass organization and movement it helps to build will be "pure" and strictly anti-Establishment in character. But there has never been a "pure" mass movement in history and there never will be, just as Lenin pointed out to purists in his own day that there has never been a "pure" revolution.*

Lynd believes that the Left of the Thirties built the mass organizations on a reformist basis and hence made it easier for the ruling class and its lackeys to either take them over or destroy them when the time came. But these mass organizations were not "creatures" of the Communist Party, as we have tried to indicate. Had the Communists just set out to build "pure" Left unions, they would have been isolated and their small unions wiped out in the mass surge toward unionism. This actually happened in a few industries, such as ladies garment and coal mining, where Left unions were inundated when the tide of mass unionization came in.

This is related to something else. Seeing the growing irrationality of the capitalist system, intellectuals increasingly transcend it in thought and arrive at socialist convictions. This is one of the most positive developments of our time and is bound to grow as the crisis of the system deepens. But if this consciousness is not related to the Marxist recognition that the material class struggle is the main motive force of history and that intellectuals must help serve that struggle, it easily gets lost in its own idealist abstractions. This expresses itself in an intellectualized view of the struggle as existing solely in the realm of consciousness. It finds its most developed form in Charles H. Reich's *The Greening of America*, which sees a war between different "levels of consciousness" to be won in an arena of abstract consciousness and not in the concrete arena of struggle against the ruling class and its system. No wonder this book won such acclaim and

---

*"Whoever expects to see a 'pure' social revolution will *never* live to see it. Such a person pays lip-service to revolution without understanding what revolution is" (Lenin, "The Discussion of Self-Determination Summed Up," p. 356).

publicity. It is as if sections of the ruling class had said: "We too are ready to buy your new level of consciousness, so long as you stay away from touching our material possessions."

But the only way the masses can learn the true nature of the capitalist system and the need to replace it—and the possibility for so doing!—is in the course of their own concrete struggle against existing property relations and the governmental power behind them. And this can never be achieved without the experience that comes from organization, an experience that teaches ordinary people a sense of their own potential power. Eugene V. Debs knew this well; so did William Z. Foster. Debs used to say that this is an age of organization and the only way the organized might of capital can be fought is by the conscious organized might of the people.

It is interesting to see the emphasis placed on the importance of organizing the people "in some way" by the Vietnamese Communists who, we must all admit, know something about the art of revolution. Le Duan, the First Secretary of the Vietnam Workers Party (Communist Party) has emphasized that:

On the road to the seizure of power the only weapon available to the masses in the revolution is organization. The hallmark of the revolutionary movement led by the proletariat is its high organizational standard. All activities that bring the masses to the point where they will rise up and overthrow the ruling classes are based on this principle: to organize, organize, organize. The purpose of political propaganda and agitation is indeed to organize the masses. Only by organizing them in some way will conditions be created for educating them and building up the immense strength of the revolution. Once organized, their power will significantly increase (Le Duan, *The Vietnamese Revolution*).

Many young radicals would agree with Le Duan that "organize, organize, organize, in some way," may be good for Vietnam, but they are not so sure about it for the United States. They fear that this country is so wealthy that the ruling class can bribe and coopt every organized movement for partial demands (reforms). The only thing they believe it cannot coopt is the slogan, "Revolution." But in this latter respect they are dead wrong. Revolutionary rhetoric is the easiest thing to coopt because it costs the ruling class nothing. Look at the way Nixon billed his 1971 grandiose Cabinet reshuffling scheme and phony revenue juggling act as "a new American Revolution—a peaceful revolution in which power has been turned back to the people"; "a revolution as profound, as far-reaching, as exciting, as that first revolution almost 200 years ago"—no less! The only way the people, therefore, can distinguish between "revolution" that is just rhetoric, "revolution" that is pure demagogy, and "revolution" that means what it says, is in getting down to the basics—what it means in their daily lives and struggle experiences.

What about the fear of cooption? It is a justified fear. The American ruling class has had the means by which to rekindle reformist illusions in the system and to absorb reform struggles. However, we do not believe that it will have the same possibilities for doing this in the period ahead as it has had this past quarter of a century. A new, entirely different period is now opening.

Yet it would be a mistake to depend upon objective conditions exclusively to ward off the danger of cooption. This was one of the errors made in the Thirties. This writer can only speak for himself. He recalls his own thinking then, as the depression dragged on year after year. He believed those conditions had become chronic for the system and would compel the masses to come in ever sharper collision with the ruling class and its institutions. Developments did not turn out exactly that way. The war intervened and "solved" the economic depression. After the war new conditions arose, including the conscious policy of the ruling class to use large-scale government intervention in the economy to flatten the economic cycle. The contradictions of the system led to a series of deep war and social crises, but not to the depression conditions that typified the decade of the Thirties.

This therefore poses a dilemma. The fight for reforms, whether economic or political, opens the door to reformist thinking; but to fail to fight for them closes the door to a mass movement. How is this enigma to be solved? Can reforms be fought for in a revolutionary way? The answer to this question is central to a correct approach to strategy.

3. Reform and Revolution

ONE COMMON error made by the new radicals who fear cooption is to pick and choose the issues and demands of immediate struggle with an eye to avoiding those that can be won. They fear winning worse than losing. They think that losing will heighten revolutionary consciousness, while winning will strengthen reformist illusions. But the American people are practical. They will fight in a mass, sustained way for things that are important *to them* and that they believe can be won either fully or in part. Even revolutions are fought around concrete needs, not abstract slogans. The Russian Socialist Revolution, for example, was fought around the slogans of Peace, Bread, Land. It was for these simple things that the Kerensky bourgeois regime was overthrown.

Slogans and demands must articulate real needs. If radicals forget this, if they merely try to impose what they think is revolutionary, they will build no real movement. People will look upon them as sloganeers and manipulators.

Le Duan, in the report previously cited, makes an exceedingly important observation:

One should not hold the oversimplified view that economic slogans are reformist while only political ones are revolutionary. There can be political slogans with a reformist character, and economic ones that carry a revolutionary content. The decision is based on the occasion, context and aim of a given slogan. A genuinely revolutionary party decisively devoted to the final goal of the revolution can, in one way or another, put the seal of the revolution on all slogans and forms of organization and struggle, including the least political ones, necessary for unifying the masses in a situation not yet favorable for all-out revolutionary actions (Le Duan, p. 44).

An example of this can be seen in the struggle for women's liberation. The demands being raised by the women's movement are essentially democratic and reformist in character. From a theoretical point of view it is even conceivable that they could be met within the confines of the present system. And from a practical point of view some of them will be, to one extent or another. This already can be seen in respect to the demand for legal abortions. But the net impact of this struggle for women's rights is not reformist. The reason for this is that the status of women is related to the nature of the system itself. The demands being raised are directed to the system as such. So long as this movement does not permit itself to become diverted into a war between the sexes and recognizes that oppressed women have more in common with *all* those oppressed and exploited by capitalism, including men, than with the women of the exploiting class, it can be of great revolutionary importance. One or another partial demand of women can be won under capitalism, but their complete liberation and freedom can never be won short of the social revolution and the building of a classless communist society.

In other words, there are no abstractly good or bad slogans or demands, although we are sure that Le Duan does not overlook the important art of selecting the more appropriate slogans and demands for each period of struggle. But he stresses that even the best slogan can serve reformist ends if not seen and fought for correctly.

In this respect there is something to be learned from the experience of the Thirties. The Communists of that period issued mountains of material propagating socialist views. But because the intensely bitter struggles were over specific, concrete demands of the people, a separation developed between ultimate goal and the immediate struggle. This became even more pronounced when concessions were won, for these fed certain illusions. Nor could this gap be bridged by resorting to revolutionary rhetoric. That was not the answer.

How then can the seal of revolution, in the words of Le Duan, be put on all slogans and demands "including the least political ones?" Part of the answer has emerged from the new radicalism of the Sixties. The slogan "Power!" has arisen from all sections of the Movement. "Black Power," "Brown Power," "Indian Power," "Consumer Power," "Woman Power," and so forth. These have all merged into the more general one of "People's Power," or "Power to the People." At present these slogans are largely rhetoric, although they raise the central political question and indicate a growing awareness that power in our society lies elsewhere than in the hands of the people.

The way to avoid both the danger of reformism and that of an abstract rhetoric divorced from the daily life and needs of the people, is to link the slogan of power with that of immediate demands in an integral and dynamic fashion. Every struggle should be seen as one with power and for power. Every specific issue and demand should be related to the question of power—who has it, how it is being used, in whose interests, and how it can and will be used if ever more effective counter power is not mustered to block it.

Without this, even concessions gained one day can be lost the next. A wage increase is won, but if the employers have a free hand to raise prices or increase speed-up, or through the government to increase taxes on working people, the wage gain is purely ephemeral. Thus the issue of a wage raise cannot be seen in isolation, but in its fuller political and class relations, its relations to those who hold and wield power. The same is true of demands put to government. Who is to pay for these? Which class? By making the people pay for social legislation through an increase in taxes the ruling class feathers its own profit nest and divides the people into warring groups—small homeowners, for example, blaming poor people on welfare for rising taxes instead of those profiteering from war, inflation and poverty.

If the Left keeps this in mind all the time and relates the question of power to the daily struggle in a concrete way, each battle, whether won or lost, can be politicized. It can be shown to be part of a larger class war that can only end when those who today hold the power are divested of it. And when victories are scored, these need not lead to confidence in the system, but a greater sense of confidence and insight into the immense latent power of the people still to be tapped.

4. Centralism vs Decentralism

IN HIS projections for the Seventies, Staughton Lynd envisions a "confederation of local mass organizations which will still be a decentralized 'movement' but which will no longer be made up largely of students and academics" ("A Program for Post-Campus Radicals"). He notes that local organizing is now being seriously undertaken in many communities and believes that some exchange of experiences of work in white communities would be helpful.

This is all to the good, but is it good enough? First, why limit such exchanges only to experiences in "white communities?" We assume that Lynd expects that the experiences of work in Black or Brown communities will be exchanged within these movements. But is there not a need also for a joint exchange of experiences? Is there not an interrelation between what is done in each community? It is wrong to believe that the Movement *must* be divided along racial lines now and that somehow, willy-nilly, unity will occur somewhere up ahead. While affirming the need for special approaches to people, we believe that the struggle for unity across racial lines cannot be postponed to the indefinite future. It must find concrete expression in what we do *all the time.*

This question is one of fundamental importance. Racism is the main ideology of the ruling class for splitting the working class along racial lines and for justifying to whites the double exploitation and oppression of Black and colored peoples. Thus the struggle against racism is central to the problem of class unity. More than that, in the United States the strategic allies of the working class in the struggle for socialism are the oppressed nationalities and, in the first place, the Black people. Thus for both reasons the question of white-Black unity is of paramount importance.

Few on the Left would dispute this. Yet over recent years a point of view has developed which says that the Blacks should organize themselves separately from whites and that whites should organize themselves separately from Blacks and then strive for unity between both organized masses.

There is something wrong here. The reason why Blacks seek to organize separately is because of white racism, because they are excluded or discriminated against by whites. Were there no racism among white workers, for example, there would be no need for Black caucuses in trade unions. Employer and union leadership racist practices would have been fought by *all* the workers as a united class. But because this is not the situation, Black workers must form their own special organizational instruments to defend their own special interests even within the framework of the same unions.

It is therefore understandable why Blacks, or Chicanos, or Puerto Ricans, as oppressed peoples, should want to form their own organizations and movements to fight for their own liberation. But white people have no reason to organize themselves as whites, except to continue the exclusion of Blacks, or Chicanos, or Puerto Ricans. Therefore it is essential that radical-minded whites do everything in their power to help bring whites and Blacks together and to fight the very concept of "white communities" and "white organizations."

There is a lesson to learn from the Thirties. In the drive to organize the new industrial unions, there were those who were ready to organize the whites separately as a matter of expediency. The Communists fought against this. Even in the heart of the racist South, where segregation was the law, the Communists refused to organize white workers if this meant organizing them in "white locals" and segregating the Black workers to "Black locals." Despite the difficulties this created, and often the sharpest animosity of white workers, in the long run this principled stand made it possible to organize the new unions in basic industry along interracial lines. It is too bad that the expulsion of the Communists from leading positions in the CIO during the Cold War hysteria of the late Forties cut short further progress in the fight for the rights of the Black workers in industry and in the unions.

The same principles apply to the organization of women. Suffering special forms of oppression *as women*, they too seek and need their own special organizations and movement through which to conduct their struggle. The rapidity with which women's liberation groups and periodicals have sprung up in recent years is one of the most healthy developments of our time. The issue of women's liberation has been firmly planted on the agenda of struggle. But where men seek to organize themselves exclusively as men the purpose and net effect is reactionary. Its aim is to exclude women and thereby perpetuate the notion of male superiority and the practice of holding women in an inferior and subordinate status.

Let us return to a discussion of centralism versus decentralism. It is not enough to have a movement made up of local mass organizations that relate to each other in only a loose decentralized way. Far more is needed. The United States is not a loosely knit confederation of semi-autonomous principalities. It is not a country of self-sufficient agrarian economies engaged in a simple form of commodity exchange. It is the land with the very highest concentration of capital in the world, whose tentacles stretch into every continent. It is this that explains the ever greater concentration of political power, not only in Washington, but in the hands of the Presidency. At a time in history replete with crises, the ruling class wants assurance of prompt effective response to every domestic or international crisis or sign of crisis. And it is this too that explains institutions like the Pentagon, the CIA, the FBI, and the qualitatively new role of government in the nation's economy.

To think that this immense concentration of economic and political power can be beaten by a series of local skirmishes, without a centralized, coordinated national plan, without a strategic deployment of human and material resources for the attainment of specific objectives, is to underestimate the foe while fooling oneself. It is repeatedly to recreate the very errors that led to the crisis of the new radicalism.

True, bureaucratic *over*-centralization is a menace, but the answer to it is not a loose *de*-centralization. Extreme tends to feed extreme. During the first years of the new radicalism there was much talk about "participatory democracy." In its most extreme form this completely negated the need for leadership. Leaders were expected to be silent when a proposal was discussed for fear that their greater prestige would influence unduly, even tend to manipulate. When this cult of unleadership ran its full course it was replaced with its opposite—a glorification of the role of the individual and of small elitist groups. The day of the Weatherman had come.

There is no such thing as unleaders, only good leaders or bad leaders. So-called unleaders also lead, but in the wrong direction. There has never been a real movement or revolution in history without leadership. Lenin, who knew a little about this, wrote: "Not a single class in history has achieved power without producing its political leaders, its prominent representatives able to organize a movement and to lead it" ("The Urgent Tasks of Our Movement," p. 370). Lenin was speaking, of course, of the need for a revolutionary vanguard. Events have more than confirmed his judgment.

But even without touching the question of a vanguard at this point, experience has shown that some form of centralism is also a necessity for the movement at large. The very local organizations that Lynd wants to see built will not long survive as purely local movements. We recall the arguments made by the SDS radical organizing caucus at the ill-fated New Politics Convention held in Chicago in the summer of 1967. It strongly opposed the formation of an independent national political movement to launch a third ticket or party in 1968 because it said this would interfere with local organizing. Without arguing the matter of electoral politics at this point, the question still arises: How much real local organizing actually took place, and where are the local groups that were formed?

People are more and more aware that the most important decisions affecting their lives are being made elsewhere. Every important local issue is today tied with a thousand strings to power structures and bureaucratic agencies outside the given locality itself. The time has come to face up to this reality. In the recent period the tendency toward provincialism has become even more pronounced. Many young radicals have retreated into their own little local collectives in the hope that somehow, by digging away in their small plots, they will find the golden bonanza everyone is looking for, the answers to all the problems of the Movement. We fear they will not be found in that way.

We are not minimizing the importance of local organizing. It is

key. In the last analysis there can be no organizing of any kind
that does not start with building where the people live and work.
But without a perspective and a plan, without a clearer vision of
what is needed to confront the Beast, local organizing will result
in some worthwhile experiences and also in a great deal of
frustration and demoralization.

We need a broader concept of organizing. We need organizations of both a vertical and horizontal type; organizations based
on community but also those that are based on issues and
concerns that cross community lines. There is an imperative need
to find ways to organize the ghettos and barrios block by block,
into tight fists of resistance and offensive struggle. There is need
for organizing the tens of millions of workers still unorganized, so
many of whom are in the lower pay categories. There is a need to
help organize all on welfare, the senior citizens on social security,
the tenants and small home owners, the women as women, the
students, college and high school, the various professional group-
ings, the consumers, and so forth. And there is need also to do
independent "organizing" inside of many established organizations, as the Left in the church movement has shown.

5. Building An Independent Mass Movement

THUS, THERE is no dearth of organizing to be done. But this
cannot be viewed as a number of separate projects each unto
itself, even though each has its own particular focus. These
should be seen as parts of a greater whole, a common nationwide
movement.

The fact is that while there is much organizing to be done, there
is much sporadic radical organization that exists. This is a period
of great ferment. Movements and organizations spring up like
mushrooms. The militant women's movement that seemed to
appear out of thin air is an example. But as we pointed out earlier,
these come and go; here today and gone tomorrow. The most
important task before the Left at this time, in our opinion, is to
find the ways and means by which to begin to link up the
thousands of spontaneous, sporadic, organized, semi-organized

and unorganized struggles, and the many movements of one kind or another that exist, into one vast unified independent political movement. The objective should be to tie these disparate efforts into a common strategic approach which singles out where the main blow should be concentrated at a given time and the relationship of immediate objectives to longer range goals.

The need for this arises from life itself. Not a single one of the burning issues of the day can be solved by itself alone. They impinge upon one another because they all arise from the basic crisis of the system itself. They can no longer be solved piecemeal or by themselves. If the fight for adequate welfare, for example, is separated from the fight against the war and militarism, it only heightens the fear of workers and middle-class people that the burden will be placed on them in higher taxes. Nor can the urban crisis and all the related social crises be solved in the old way of liberal reform. New radical approaches are necessary. Structural changes are needed, even if the slightest meaningful improvements are going to be made. The problem of ecology is a case in point. The fact is that only socialism can be the solution for all these multiple crises. A movement that is politically independent, which aims to coordinate and bring together all the areas of discontent and protest into a mighty torrent of struggle, may not be a movement for socialism at the outset, but objectively it must move in that direction. Especially will this be so if those who are revolutionists help to inspire and organize this movement and try to guarantee from the outset that above all it remains truly independent.

It is this that is so lacking today. There is a Movement, we have referred to it in these pages numerous times, and yet in a deeper sense there is no *real* movement. There is no unified mass independent force that confronts the system and its government with a meaningful challenge and the nation with a meaningful alternative program and course of action.

Until such a coordinated independent political force arises, the Movement will continue to remain in swaddling clothes. We are not speaking of a *monolithic* movement, but a *coordinated* movement. How to begin to build such a movement, as a real and not a mere rhetorical challenge to power, is the first and most important problem confronting all of us on the Left.

Without making such a transition, the crisis of the new radicalism and of the Left as a whole will not abate. The gap between what is needed to take the next leap forward and the provincial immaturity of the Movement in its present form will only add frustration upon frustration. The Movement cannot stand still. It must make the transition to a higher form of organization and consciousness or find itself trapped in deeper and deeper crisis.

There are increasing signs that sections of the Movement are begining to move, hesitantly though it be, in this new direction. There is now discussion about the need for "coalition," a word considered taboo only a few years ago. There is a recognition that peace is closely related to the vital questions of domestic concern and that the Movement, therefore, can no longer be just single-issued or just academia oriented. There is a conscious effort to coalesce organizations and movements representing different mass constituencies around multi-issue programs. These are healthy and important beginnings. What is still lacking is the full consciousness of where this must head.

The split in the national peace movement that occured in 1970 was partly over this issue. There are some who want to keep each issue hermetically separated from the others. They refuse to link the issue of the war to its domestic consequences. They want the racism perpetrated against the Indochinese people to be separated from the racism perpetrated at home. They want Blacks alone to fight for Black freedom, Chicanos along to fight for Chicano freedom, and that the "white Movement" remain aloof from these struggles. And this is argued in the name of keeping the Movement "broad." While we favor mustering the largest support around separate issues as can be attained, the task of those who consider themselves revolutionists, or even advanced progressives, is to *politicize* the struggle, which means to show people the *inter-relationship* of issues and how they are joined together in life itself.

The task of building such a unified, politically independent mass movement is exceedingly complicated. It will not arise overnight. It will never arise if there is no conscious struggle for it. It must be worked for and fought for. It has become urgent. In fact, it is long overdue. Not only the fate of the Movement but that of the country and the world may well hinge on our ability to build such a movement. The present impasse cannot long remain frozen. It will be broken one way or the other. Either the country will be moved to peace and in the direction of socialism, or it will be dragged to an American form of military-fascist-racist rule and the threat of a world holocaust.

To begin means to consciously and actively work for the linking-up of struggles and movements through mutual support, common actions, integrated programs and a one-for-all, all-for-one spirit. While stressing the fact that such a movement must be conceived of as nationwide in character, it must be built locally, regionally and nationally at one and the same time. Already local coalitions that unite sectors of the militant Movement are springing up in different parts of the country. As these develop and multiply they feed the currents of national coalition, while agreement between national organizations and movements helps stimulate the process of local unity. Certainly at a time of mass struggle and repression, when there are literally thousands of political prisoners and frame-ups and trials in every part of the country, there is tremendous need for coordinated, joint, united efforts on every level.

6. Electoral Politics

A MOVEMENT that is politically independent is by its nature a political movement, if by political is meant the conscious attempt to alter power relations in society. This is so whether such a movement engages in electoral politics or not. The direct mass struggle of the people has always been more important than the electoral struggle per se. Even in the Thirties, it was the great mass militant struggles of the unemployed, workers, farmers and youth that set the tone for the period. Whatever concessions were won came as a result of these. Of course, as a consequence of these struggles more liberal candidates took the field, won elections and then got the credit for reforms. Just as today, the war in Indochina can be brought to an end by the action of Congress. Yet it is quite clear that if Congress took this course it would not be because of election results alone, but because of the great mass revulsion to the war and the organized mass movement of militant struggle against it.

Yet as soon as a movement really sinks roots and begins to relate to the needs of ordinary people it cannot evade the question of electoral politics. When the coal miners began their great militant movement for protection from the black lung disease, it soon swept over into the electoral arena. The same is true of the movement of Black people in the South for the control of their own local communities. And even when such participation is not undertaken by the movement itself, certain individuals associated with the movement proceed to enter the race for office. The election of Ron Dellum to Congress from the Berkeley-Oakland area of California, and of Bella Abzug in the 19th Congressional District of New York, are examples of this. Thus this issue is bound to arise wherever a real movement exists. And now with the 18-year-old vote won, it is sure to arise in university towns and districts on a scale not witnessed previously.

Two types of arguments are made against electoral participation. The first is the anarchist philosophical objection to doing anything that seems to sanction the existence of State power. But as we have discussed previously, the State is not just a state of mind. It will not disappear by mere civil disobedience. The capitalist State will cease to exist when it is replaced by a socialist State. This can only be the result of the revolutionary action of the people. For this they must first become convinced that the present State is an organ of repression directed against them, that its democracy is hollow, and that it cannot be made into their own.

The second type of argument is political. It is opposed to electoral participation on the ground that it inevitably sows reformist illusions and the belief that society can be revolutionized by means of the ballot.

Parliamentary illusions are not to be discounted. This is exactly where Social-Democracy went off the deep end. But these illusions do exist and the question is how to counter them. Lenin pointed out, "*all*, positively all methods of struggle in bourgeois society . . . if left to the spontaneous course of events, become frayed, corrupted and prostituted." Strikes, he wrote, become corrupted into agreements between employers and workers "*against* the consumers." Parliaments become corrupted "into brothels," and newspapers become corrupted "into public pimps, into a means of corrupting the masses, of pandering to the low instincts of the mob, and so forth and so on." The *only* thing that can prevent such corruption, Lenin stressed, is the ennobling influence of socialist consciousness ("Guerrilla Warfare," p. 92). It all depends therefore on how this form of struggle is viewed. Lenin and the Russian Bolsheviks certainly had no parliamentary illusions. They knew that tsarism could not be overthrown by means of the ballot box. Yet they participated actively in elections and had their own bloc of deputies in the tsarist State Duma (national parliament). But these deputies were chosen not for the votes they would cast but to play the role of "tribunes of the people," to use parliament itself as the forum from which to expose the system and educate the people for revolutionary struggle.

In his book *"Left-Wing" Communism*, Lenin argued against Communists who opposed participating in bourgeois elections because they believed parliamentarism to be dead. Lenin wrote that so long as any considerable mass of people still have illusions in the system, parliamentarism "is not yet politically obsolete" and "participation in parliamentary elections and in the struggle in parliament is obligatory." This is necessary, continued Lenin, precisely to help educate the backward strata and to awaken and enlighten the mass. "As long as you are unable to disperse the bourgeois parliament and every other type of reactionary institution, you *must* work inside them." Otherwise, warned Lenin, "you run the risk of becoming babblers" (p. 42).

The great mass of the American people are untouched by Left thinking and all too frequently view it as if it were a strange creature from some other planet. A conscious decision on the part of the Left of this country to participate in the electoral struggle as a united force—or as near united as possible—would be of profound significance. It would do more than anything else to begin to end an esoteric kind of existence. It would compel the Left to confront the political spokesmen of the bourgeoisie in the arena of public debate with the aim of exposing and isolating them. It would compel election debates to begin to deal with questions of substance, not only in respect to the war and the garrison state being built, but the character of the system as a whole. It would also compel the Left to take stock of itself, to begin to relate to the needs of the people and to speak a language devoid of sectarianism, flamboyancy, or rhetoric.

Without this, the growing discontent so visible among all sections of the people and the mounting feeling that something is basically wrong somewhere, cannot be counted on automatically to swell the ranks of the Left. It could lead to an immense accretion of ultra-Right influence and power. The ten million votes cast for George Wallace in 1968 were not all cast by dyed-in-the-wool racist reactionaries. Many were cast by people deeply troubled, seeking some radical change, and swayed by the populist demagogy of Wallace.* If the Left never even tries to communicate with them how can this be prevented?

*In the 1968 election campaign Wallace issued a brochure to working people with the slogan, "The Workingman Is the Hope of America."

CHAPTER X

MORE ON STRATEGY

1. The Labor Movement

WHAT MAKES a discussion of the need for a politically independent peoples' mass movement seem far-fetched at this time, is the realization that without a firm base in the ranks of the working class such a movement cannot really shape up and if it does, cannot reach first base. This recognition of the decisive importance of the working-class movement expresses itself in two seemingly opposite ways. On the part of some there is an attitude of total despair. They see no chance of change and hide their despondency in individualistic acts and rhetoric, which all too frequently turn into passivity. Others, have a "waiting for Lefty" approach, which is also a form of passivity.

The question of the working class, therefore, is at the hub of all problems that we face. There is a paradox also in the fact that the working class is by no means unorganized. True, only a portion of it is organized into trade unions. But this mass is by no means small; it consists of some 17 million working people. Also, while we have spoken of organizations and movements that live a sporadic kind of existence, the labor movement is a stable form of organization. This is one of the characteristics of its strength, but it is also a reason for its lethargy on some questions and its general slowness to move to new terrains of struggle. And its very firm institutionalization makes it easier prey to bureaucratic control and corruption. Yet the organized labor movement represents the most important organized mass of people in the country.

Some of the negative aspects of the present-day labor movement arise precisely from the fact that it is so important an organized mass. If this were not the case the employing class would not bother to keep the labor movement in line and to buy off its leaders with bourgeois respectability.

There was a time when labor unions had to fight for their right to exist every inch of the way. That they are now accepted indicates that the ruling class has learned to live with them and to use them to maintain work discipline and to put reins on spontaneous "wild-cat" work stoppages. But this is only one side of the matter. Power respects power. The ruling class recognizes the tremendous potential power inherent in organized labor. In every labor dispute both sides of this equation are present— employer recognition that they must concede something to the power of organized labor and that *if* they do they can use it to help maintain the normal production rhythm necessary for high profit-making.

Labor leadership also understands this. No matter how corrupt it may be, it knows that it must deliver something to the workers or be unable to play its chosen role of employing-class lackey. It, too, therefore, respects the fact that the workers are conscious at least of their negative power as a united mass, the power to disrupt profitmaking by halting production. And when labor leadership forgets this and becomes smug in its belief that it can control the workers, their power to disrupt production bursts forth with elemental fury.

The equilibrium established in the "labor contract" is constantly under challenge at the point of production by *both* sides, each trying to win certain advantages for itself. At regular and sometimes irregular intervals it is violently ruptured and must be reestablished again on a somewhat new footing. Thus the relationship is always tenuous, always fraught with tension, never to be depended upon with certainty. In other words, hidden or muffled though it may be, the class struggle continues unabated wherever men and women sell their labor power in order to live.

Proof of this can be seen in a simple fact. As trustworthy as are most labor officials in defense of the system, the ruling class cannot depend upon them alone. It must use its governmental power to establish limits on the right to strike and to hem the workers in with legal technicalities. In recent years more and more so-called "labor laws" have been passed that are in reality anti-labor laws. The president and Congress have also assumed the power to halt strikes that endanger "national security," a phrase so broad as to give them the right to halt any major strike they want to. Solidarity strikes and boycott actions are also now illegal, and Rube Goldberg-like grievance procedures ensnare the workers in a legal web so intricate as to produce nothing but endless frustration.

When times are relatively good for the ruling class, and when the labor market is tight, worker-boss relations are more "peaceful." This is so even when more strikes may occur. In periods of inflation, for example, when the employers believe they can write off a wage increase by an even larger price rise, they still try to whittle the increase down, but the battle itself is kept within certain agreed upon, prescribed bounds. Under such circumstances a strike may even be desired by employers as a pretext to raise prices or reduce inventory.

But when the profit picture is not so bright, when there is greater competition from other industries or from abroad, when growing unemployment begins to replace a tight labor market, or when inflation must be curbed by an attempt to hold wages down, then the struggle tends to sharpen and strikes become more protracted and bitter. Every demand of the workers for more pay is met by the demand of the employers for increased production. There is greater pressure for the introduction of new labor-saving machines and for increased speed-up to lower the cost of production per unit at the expense of the working class. We have now entered a period of that kind. Wage increases are no longer keeping pace with rising prices and taxes. On-the-job tension increases and with it the rate of industrial accidents and fatalities. Thus a new mood is beginning to develop in labor's ranks, especially among the young. They are affected by the radical mood of their generation, by the war in Vietnam, because many of them are Black, Chicano or Puerto Rican, and because as youth they do not fear the loss of pension or have the same kind of fear of losing their jobs.

During the negotiations between the Ford Motor Company and the United Auto Workers, revealing stories of this new mood appeared in the Detroit press. One of these reads:

Ford Motor Co., and the UAW negotiators spent the day Wednesday discussing the problem of absenteeism in the plants—a new and serious problem caused by a new breed of factory worker whom both the union and the company are trying to understand.

Ford gave the UAW examples of men who were not sick being absent on long medical leaves and of assembly lines shutting down for minutes, hours and days because not enough men showed up to operate them (*Detroit Free Press*, August 20, 1970).

Sidney McKenna, chairman of Ford's negotiating team "blamed high rates of absenteeism on the 'younger employee whose environment and social background is so different from a generation ago.' He said that the new young employee is not a clock watcher and is often late for work."

James Roche, chairman of General Motors, complained that the rate of absenteeism is "twice as high as a few years ago." GM's rate is 6 per cent and as high as 13 per cent on Mondays and Fridays.

At the Chrysler Eldon plant a "Memo of Understanding" was drawn up between management and labor leadership to deal with this situation. It was adopted by a majority of 70 votes out of 670 cast, with most stewards and local executive board members voting against (*RPM*, Vol. 1, No. 3, 1970).

Thus the situation is changing and will change far more. Those who do not see this are making the same mistake made by many in the 1950s. They erroneously concluded that the "silent generation" was the forerunner of successive silent generations and that "the end of ideology had come." This uneven development of the struggle is not strange. Lenin noted that "Capitalism is not so harmoniously built that the various springs of rebellion can immediately merge of their own accord without reverses or defeats" ("The Discussion on Self-Determination Summed Up," p. 162.)

We do not want to oversimplify the problem. There is an encrusted bureaucracy in the labor movement that will have to be pushed aside. This will not be easy. Furthermore, the pattern of the attack on the standard of living is more complicated than in the past. In the late Twenties and early Thirties, great spontaneous labor struggles broke forth in response to direct wage-cutting assaults of the employers. Now the attacks are more concealed, more indirect. On the surface the workers seem to be increasing their income, and in paper dollars they are. But in relation to prices and taxes they are falling behind. Thus the struggle is not just with the given employer. It is now more of a direct political struggle. And for this the workers must fight as *a class,* not just on the picket line.

The process of change is therefore slower, but in many ways can become of greater overall class significance than in the past. It would be a tragic mistake if young radicals did not relate to what is happening to the workers and did not play a role in helping to bring this greater political class understanding to them.

There are some in the new radicalism who say, "Yes, the workers can and must be won, but it is hopeless to think you can change the unions." Young radicals of the Twenties and early Thirties felt the same way. The unions then were made up of only highly skilled craft workers. The leadership of these unions was no whit less reactionary than the present one. Yet a great explosion came that in a few years brought a new fresh breeze through labor's ranks.

Some argue, "So what, look where the trade unions are today." But the starting point of a new labor upheaval will be where the other left off. The fact that there are some 17 million workers in trade unions today and that the most powerful of them are industrial unions, is by no means a negative fact. As the struggle grows it must affect these unions for there is no other way in which the economic struggle can be waged. Workers may not attend a union meeting for years, but when they know that something important is coming up that vitally affects them they will flock to the meeting by the thousands. As much as they may detest or distrust union leaders they recognize that without the unions they are helpless. Those in the new radicalism who run away from the hard job of working inside the trade unions in the hope of finding some better "pure" form of labor organization will fail as have all such efforts in the past.

To make radical changes in the trade union movement requires that a new generation of workers, particularly young radicals, have a clear concept of what they want to achieve, what class-struggle trade unionism should be. In the Thirties, the industrial form of organization was the new unionism of that day. Because it was new and arose out of fierce, unrelenting struggle with the employing class, it was more democratic and rank-and-file based than the old type craft unionism. Today, too, it remains a superior form of unionism, for the workers do not think of themselves in just narrow craft terms, but as workers of a given plant or industry.

But even this newer form of trade unionism has permitted its role to become blunted and warped and to degenerate. It is necessary, therefore, to think of a new unionism for today that does not concentrate so much on *form* as on *content,* and arises from the new conditions and needs of the struggle. In fact, young radicals should work for an entirely new vision of unionism.

The starting place for change is with the workers themselves in their shop, department, office or workplace. The most important thing here is the revitalization of the shop steward system and grievance procedure. Most grievances should be settled by the workers right on the job and they should have the right to shut down production in support of their demands where this is necessary. The workers in each department and plant should aim to establish their own control over the speed of production and work norms, over the right to introduce new machinery, and over safety regulations.

The new vision of unionism that militants should fight for must aim to wipe out every vestige of racist discrimination in the workplace *and in the union.* It should fight to guarantee full equality for all minority, women and young workers. Union leaders should be forbidden by their members from investing union funds in corporation stocks or giving loans or entering into other business relations with the employers in their industry or any industry. Salaries of union officials should be in line with the top wages of workers in the given industry and not with those of corporation executives. Union officials should be required to return to the work bench periodically so that they are less removed from the problems and the thinking of workers on the job.

Unions should also be made to react to the many issues of social crisis that affect their members and the nation. When labor-saving machinery is introduced, the union cannot be concerned only with its own members on the job, but with the effects of this on the next generation as well. It should fight for a shorter work week without reduction in take-home pay as the most important of all demands in the struggle against the effects of automation. The 40-hour week should be considered as the maximum work week and the 30-hour week as the normal one.

Workers should also be concerned with whether a pay increase comes out of company profits or is passed on to the consumers (the workers) in the form of higher prices. The responsibility of unions to the general welfare should be part of a new unionism. Painters, for example, should concern themselves with the ways and means of eliminating the lead poisoning that takes young lives in our ghettos and barrios every year. Construction workers should demand work on housing for the people instead of more commercial skyscrapers. Workers should concern themselves with whether their plants add to water or air pollution and be ready to expose the culpability of the corporations in this matter. Auto workers should expose faulty mechanisms that endanger people's lives. Transport workers should lead the fight for free rapid urban transportation as a public service. Unions should demand reconversion of war plants for peaceful purposes and should submit the plans for such. Unions should be prepared to speak up for the poor, the aged, the young, the sick and the handicapped.

A new generation of workers should compel the unions to think along new lines. This means to improve the fight on the job against exploitation. But it also means a political fight against the politics of exploitation and against the two-party political structure of the employing class. And the workers should insist that their unions be in the forefront of the fight against war and imperialist aggression.

We know that this view of militant unionism is not the one practiced today. And we also know that young militants who seek that kind of unionism have to begin with much lesser issues than many of those mentioned here. But the unions have become so bureaucratized over the past quarter of a century that many workers do not even have a concept of what to fight for. Even where "young Turks" want to upset a leadership, they often do not know what to put in its place. Let us take the Miners Union as an example. Even if the corrupt Boyle machine is ousted, what kind of unionism would replace it if a challenge is not made to the union's present practice of owning banks in Washington and of investing miners' money in coal corporations! This is why young people must have a vision of a different kind of unionism.

We have no illusion about how rapidly changes will occur on the top. But we believe it is possible to make rapid changes in the thinking of workers and in the policies of shop organizations and local unions. Already many unions, including quite a number of internationals, have spoken out against the war. Here and there unions are also cooperating to help form broader coalitions of struggle. How rapidly the thinking of workers can change is to be seen among the "hard-hats." In 1970 they were seen assaulting student anti-war marchers; in 1971 some of them have been seen marching with students in protest against Nixon and the war.

The rapid growth of rank-and-file and black caucus movements in many unions is a sign of a new awakening of the workers. This has just barely begun, but change is in the air.

2. The World Controversy

THE NEW radicalism and the Left as a whole has also been divided on what position to take toward the bloc of socialist States that exists now for the first time in world history. In the Thirties the problem was simple. There was but one socialist country and nearly all on the Left understood the need to defend it from imperialism and to closely identify with it. The problem today is more complicated. With 14 socialist States in existence there is a tendency to identify more closely with one or the other of them. This has become particularly pronounced since ideolgical divisions arose between the socialist states. In fact, some on the Left have tried to apply methods of struggle of their favorite socialist country without regard to the vastly different conditions in the United States. A similar mistake was made by the Left in the Thirties.

It is obvious that as long as important differences exist in the outlook and policies of socialist countries these issues are also going to find reflection and be discussed and debated in the United States as well. This is only natural. But over and above this, it is necessary to achieve some common approach to the socialist camp as such.

It seems to this writer that a common approach could be something like this:

We view the existence of a bloc of socialist States as the most important asset of the world revolutionary movement. Whatever criticisms or disagreements we may have with the policies of one or another of them, we support them in their struggle against imperialism and for the construction of the new society. We favor friendly relations with all of them and consider that none of them, or any combination of them, in any way threatens the security or welfare of the American people.

We deplore the divisions that have arisen between socialist States and express the hope contained in the last words of the immortal Ho Chi Minh that the socialist countries and the world revolutionary movement will find the path to unity again. Regardless of ideological differences, we believe that unity of action against imperialism is imperative.

Flowing from this principled position we combat anti-communism in whatever shape or form it takes, whether it be anti-Soviet, anti-China, or anti-Cuba in its manifestation. We recognize that since the emergence of socialism as a world force the ideology of anti-communism is only next to racism the weapon of the ruling class to justify aggression abroad and to hold back the struggle for socialism in the United States.

Whether a common approach along these lines is possible we do not know. Whatever positions we hold on the international controversy, our special task is to try to apply Marxism-Leninism creatively to ever changing conditions and to the concrete characteristics and complexities of the class struggle in the United States.

3. Closing the Generation Gap

HOPEFULLY, GIVEN the beginnings of a common approach to strategy, we can start to put an end to the generational concepts of the "Old Left" and "New Left." We should return to the simpler and more accurate class designation of plain Left. The very origin of the term "Left" has nothing whatever to do with generations. It has everything to do with classes and with the economic, political and social class struggle. The Left traditionally has represented the "lower classes," i.e., the workers, poor farmers, professionals, and small merchants—those held down by the "upper classes," the landed aristocracy and the bourgeoisie. The term "Left Wing" itself arose during the French Revolution when the representatives of the "lower classes," mainly the radical petty-bourgeoisie of that time, were seated on the left side of the National Assembly chamber.

The central question of politics has been and continues to be: Which side are you on, on the side of the exploiters or on the side of the exploited? It has never been and is not now a question of being on the side of youth or on the side of age. The youth are no more homogeneous as a social formation than are the middle-aged or the old.

There is such a thing, of course, as being old-fashioned and stodgy in one's thinking. It is also true that young people are more receptive to new ideas and a new perception of things. Therefore youth will usually make up a larger proportion of the Left than any other age bracket. But not everything that parades as new is new. It may be new only in appearance, but actually conceal a content that is very old and reactionary.

If the only gap were that of age, then it would disappear automatically, for more and more of those in the "Old Left" are now young people, while many of those of the "New Left" are looked upon by the newer crop of radicals as also "Old."

But the gap arose, not from a matter of age, though it was a factor, but from ideological differences. Thus a coming together on ideological questions is the key to closing the gap.

This requires recognizing that no generation is born by immaculate conception. Each carries within it, for better or worse, the seeds of past generations. This is as true historically as it is biologically. If every generation really started from scratch in its accumulation of knowledge, we would still be back in the pre-paleolithic age. To mix metaphors a bit, each generation participates in a relay race in which it passes the torch to the next in line. Whether the previous runner was fast or slow, had gained or lost a lap, is immaterial. The new sprinter starts where the old leaves off.

As we have shown, one such runner, that of the "silent generation" of the Fifties, never really showed up. Few entered the radical race in that period and many fell by the wayside. Hence it appeared to the new activists in the early peace and civil rights struggles that there had been nothing before them; everyone had sold out; the race had to start from the beginning. And as we have shown, the postwar world was very different from that of the prewar; the experiences, slogans and movements of the Thirties, Forties, and early Fifties, seemed to the new militants like relics of a bygone age.

It was under these conditions, with the working class taking a back seat in the political fray, that the new radicalism arose and left its mark on subsequent events. It is no accident that under such circumstances many false notions of man, society and class relations took hold, and a hybrid form of anarcho-Marxism took shape. This was not the first time in world history when something like this occurred. After the defeat of the Paris Commune in 1871, Bakuninist anarchism nearly inundated the First International despite the genius of Marx and Engels. In the period of the 1880s, anarchism also arose as a significant factor in the class struggle in the United States. And in tsarist Russia at the turn of the century, Tolstoyan, populist and nihilist forms of anarchism also held considerable sway in radical-revolutionary circles. What is important to remember about each of these historic instances is that they were followed, after anarchism had been found futile, with a great upsurge of Marxist thinking and the socialist movement.

We believe that the same is going to happen now. But this is not something written in the heavens; it can only become so if the ideas of creative Marxism win out against the false theories of anarchism and become the basis for the building of a solid mass movement for revolutionary change.

We have concentrated our remarks on an *approach* to strategy, particularly the imperative need to pull together and consolidate the present amorphous and splintered Movement into a vast *independent* coordinated political movement. This will not be achieved overnight. Even in the process of realizing it new problems of program, strategy, tactical alliances, and of short and long range objectives will arise.

Lenin emphasized that the summit of revolution cannot be scaled in one swift assault. Stopping-off places, intermediary plateaus (stages), are inevitable. These cannot be foreseen in advance. They are not visible from afar. By following the Marxist method of analyzing social phenomenon in its concreteness, and by immersing itself in the daily struggles of the people, the Left will grow wings and learn to soar. From greater heights it will perceive many things that its limited vision is incapable of discerning today.

As this is being written, the struggle to end the war against the Indochinese people is central. It is integrally linked with all the burning domestic issues of crisis. When this terrible war is over, new struggles and new objectives will emerge. The struggle for a reversal of national priorities will sharpen and with it the issues of poverty, racism, and the dominance of the giant monopolies and conglomerates over the life of the nation.

This will require a revolutionary vanguard capable of moving the struggle from one stage to another without at any time losing sight of the revolutionary goal. It will require a vanguard capable of teaching the people and learning from them at the same time. And because the struggle in the United States is more complicated than anywhere else in the world, it will require a vanguard that constantly deepens its theoretical insights into the workings of modern-day state monopoly capitalism and knows how to absorb and apply creatively the lessons of *all* world revolutionary experience.

As a long time leader of the Communist Party, it is the opinion of this writer that it provides the nucleus of such a revolvutionary vanguard. Obviously this is not a view around which unity of the entire Left is as yet possible. We could agree, however, with Lenin's approach. He wrote: "For it is not enough to call ourselves the 'vanguard,' the advanced contingent; we must act in such a way that *all* the other contingents recognize and are obliged to admit that we are marching in the vanguard" (*What Is To Be Done*, p. 83).

No one knows nor can know when or under what specific conditions the socialist revolution will climax in the United States. We are convinced that it cannot be anything less than the action of the majority. Furthermore, the socialist revolution is not a mere replacement of Washington Administrations. It is a smashing of the oppressive capitalist state machinery and its replacement with a revolutionary socialist State. How much violence takes place either prior to or after the change in class rule will depend upon what measures the capitalist class employs to thwart the will of the majority.

As for socialism in the United States, it will be greatly different from elsewhere. Our great productive capacity can give abundance to all almost immediately and can rapidly replace alienated toil with creative labor and a flowering of the human personality. Most important of all, when socialism comes to the United States there will be no power on earth capable of challenging it. The death of U.S. imperialism will spell the death of world imperialism. It will herald the triumph of the world's peoples and the rebirth of the American nation.

There is no country in the world where the objective material conditions are riper for a developed socialist society than in the United States. Our economy is of such magnitude, of such high technology, so diversified and so internationalized in scope, that what is good for the world is also good for the American people. What is bad for the American people is bad for the world. In other words, the real self-interest of the overwhelming majority of this country merges with the interests of the people of the world. Instead of our nation being the curse of the world, as it now is, it could become the blessing. The great task of the Left, a task greater in magnitude and significance than for the Left of any other country, is to make this a reality.

BIBLIOGRAPHY

Bakunin, Michael, "Marxism, Freedom and the State," in Horowitz, *The Anarchists.*

Baldwin, Hanson W., "After Vietnam—What Military Strategy in the Far East?," *New York Times Magazine,* June 9, 1968.

Beard, Charles and Mary, *The Rise of the American Civilization,* Macmillan, New York, 1933, Vol. I.

Brenan, George, "Anarchism in Spain," in Horowitz, *The Anarchists.*

Castro, Fidel, "Interview," *Socialist Revolution,* Vol. 1, No. 1, 1970.

Cleaver, Eldrige, *On the Ideology of the Black Panther Party,* Published by Black Panther Party, 1970.

_____, *Soul On Ice,* Dell, New York, 1968.

Cohn-Bendit, Daniel and Gabriel, "The Battle of the Streets," in *New-Left Reader,* Carl Oglesby, *ed.,* Grove Press, New York, 1969.

Dibble, Vernon K., "The Garrison Society," *New University Thought,* Special Issue, 1966-67.

Durant, Will and Ariel, *The Reformation,* Simon & Schuster, New York, 1957.

Engels, Frederick, "Anarchism and Conspiratorial Ethics," *Basic Writings on Politics and Philosophy of Marx and Engels,* Anchor Books, New York, 1959.

_____, "Condition of the Working Class in England," in Marx and Engels, *On Britain,* Moscow, 1953.

_____, *Dialectics of Nature,* International Publishers, New York 1971.

_____, *"On Authority,"* in *Basic Writings on Politics and Philosophy of Marx and Engels,* Anchor Books, New York, 1959.

_____, *Peasant War in Germany,* International Publishers, New York, 1966.

_____, "Preface to the Communist Manifesto," in *Birth of the Communist Manifesto,* Dirk Struik, *ed.,* International Publishers, New York, 1971.

Foner, Philip S., *History of the Labor Movement in the United States,* International Publishers, New York, 1955, Vol. 2.

Foster, William Z., *History of the Communist Party of the United States,* International Publishers, New York, 1952.

_____, *History of the Three Internationals,* International Publishers, New York, 1955.

Gleason, Ralph J., "The Power of Non-Politics or the Death of the Square Left," *Evergreen Review,* September 1967.

Goodman, Paul, *Like a Conquered Province,* Random House, New York, 1967.

Guérin, Daniel, *Anarchism*, Monthly Review Press, New York, 1970.

Guevara, Ernesto Che, "Lessons of the Cuban Revolution," in *Guerrilla Warfare and Marxism*, William J. Pomeroy, *ed.*, International Publishers, New York, 1968.

Hoffman, Abbie, *Revolution for the Hell of It*, Dial, New York, 1968.

Horowitz, Irving L., *ed., The Anarchists*, Dell, New York, 1964.

Ibarruri, Dolores, *They Shall Not Pass*, International Publishers, New York, 1966.

Jacker, Corinne, *The Black Flag of Anarchism*, Scribner, New York, 1968.

Kempton, Murray, "Understanding the Police," *The New York Review of Books*, November 5, 1970.

Kennedy, John F., "Yale Commencement Address," *New York Times* June 12, 1962.

Landis, Arthur H., *The Abraham Lincoln Brigade*, Citadel Press, New York, 1967.

Le Duan, *The Vietnamese Revolution*, International Publishers, New York, 1971.

Lenin, V. I., "Differences in the European Labor Movement," *Collected Works*, Moscow, 1963, Vol. 16.

———, "The Discussion of Self-Determination Summed Up," in *National Liberation, Socialism and Imperialism,* International Publishers, New York, 1968.

———, "Guerrilla Warfare," in *Guerrilla Warfare and Marxism,* William J. Pomeroy, *ed.*, International Publishers, New York, 1968.

———, *Imperialism: The Highest Stage of Capitalism*, International Publishers, New York, 1970.

———, *"Left-Wing" Communism, an Infantile Disorder*, International Publishers, New York, 1969.

———, "Letters on Tactics," *Collected Works*, Moscow, 1964, Vol. 24.

———, "A Review of Kautsky's Book," *Collected Works*, Moscow, 1961, Vol. 4.

———, "Socialism and Anarchism," *Collected Works*, Moscow, 1962, Vol. 10.

———, "The Urgent Tasks of Our Movement," *Collected Works*, Moscow, 1961, Vol. 4.

———, *What Is To Be Done?* International Publishers, New York, 1969.

———, "Where to Begin," *Collected Works*, Moscow, 1961, Vol. 5.

Lipset, Seymour M., *The Political Man,* Anchor Books, New York, 1963.

Lynd, Staughton, "A Program for Post-Campus Radicals," *Liberation,* August-September 1969.

Marcuse, Herbert, *One-Dimensional Man*, Beacon Press, Boston, 1967.

Martin, Kingsley, "French Liberal Thought in the Eighteenth Century," in Horowitz, *The Anarchists*.

Marx, Karl, *Capital,* International Publishers, New York, 1967, Vol. 1.

_____, *Class Struggles in France,* International Publishers, New York, 1969.

Marx, Karl, and Engels, Frederick, *The Communist Manifesto,* International Publishers, New York, 1948.

_____, *Selected Correspondence,* International Publishers, New York, 1935.

Masaryk, Thomas G., "Peasant Anarchism in Russia," in Horowitz, *The Anarchists.*

Mehring, Franz, *Karl Marx,* Ann Arbor Paperbacks, 1962.

Mills, C. Wright, *The Marxists,* Dell, New York, 1962.

Nechayev, Sergei, "Catechism of a Revolutionist," in Horowitz, *The Anarchists.*

Oglesby, Carl, *Containment and Change,* Macmillan, New York, 1967.

Powell, William, *The Anarchist Cookbook,* Lyle Stuart, Inc., New York, 1971.

Reich, Charles A., *The Greening of America,* Random House, New York, 1970.

Roszak, Theodore, *The Making of a Counter Culture,* Anchor Books, New York, 1969.

Sartre, Jean-Paul, "Interview," *New Left Review,* November-December 1969.

Schlesinger, Arthur Jr., *Violence, America in the Sixties,* Signet Books, New York, 1968.

Shapiro, Karl, "On the Revival of Anarchism," *Liberation,* February 1961.

Smith, Adam, *Inquiry into the Nature and Causes of the Wealth of Nations,* Methuen, London, 1930, Vol. II.

Taylor, William W., "Unintended Consequences of Nixon's Welfare Plan," *Social Work,* October, 1970.

Tolstoy, Leo, "Gandhi-Tolstoy Correspondence," Horowitz, *The Anarchists.*

Willis, Ellen, "Consumerism and Women," *Socialist Revolution,* May-June 1970.

Wilson, Woodrow, *The New Freedom,* Doubleday, Page & Co., New York, 1913.

Winston, Henry, "Unity and Militancy for Freedom and Equality," *Political Affairs,* February 1968.

INDEX

J1